Computer Graphics and Imaging

Edited by Branislav Sobota

Published in London, United Kingdom

IntechOpen

Supporting open minds since 2005

Computer Graphics and Imaging
http://dx.doi.org/10.5772/intechopen.75340
Edited by Branislav Sobota

Contributors
Lulu Wang, Andrew Chalmers, Chao Tong, Robert S Laramee, Bulganmaa Bulgaa Togookhuu, Dean Thomas, Rita Borgo, Simon Hands, Nobuhiko Mukai, Branislav Sobota

First published in London, United Kingdom, 2019 by IntechOpen
IntechOpen is the global imprint of INTECHOPEN LIMITED, registered in England and Wales, registration number: 11086078, The Shard, 25th floor, 32 London Bridge Street
London, SE19SG – United Kingdom
Printed in Croatia

British Library Cataloguing-in-Publication Data
A catalogue record for this book is available from the British Library

Additional hard and PDF copies can be obtained from orders@intechopen.com

Computer Graphics and Imaging
Edited by Branislav Sobota
p. cm.
Print ISBN 978-1-83962-282-3
Online ISBN 978-1-83962-283-0
eBook (PDF) ISBN 978-1-83962-284-7

For EU product safety concerns:
IN TECH d.o.o., Prolaz Marije Krucifikse Kozulić 3, 51000 Rijeka, Croatia, info@intechopen.com or visit our website at intechopen.com.

Meet the editor

Branislav Sobota was born in 1967. In 1990 he graduated (MSc.) with honors at the Department of Computers and Informatics of the FEEI at the Technical University in Košice, Slovakia. He obtained his PhD in 1999 and habilitation thesis in 2008 in the field of virtual reality and computer graphics. He is currently working as an associate professor at the Department of Computers and Informatics at the Technical University of Košice, Slovakia. His scientific research is focused on computer graphics, parallel computing, and especially virtual reality and related technologies.

Contents

Preface

Human evolution is tied to the process of collecting, processing, transferring, and recording information. If people gain most of their most information visually, then computer graphics is one of the generational changes in computer technology. Creating a book on computer graphics is quite challenging given its actual range. Nevertheless, in this book, modern approaches, procedures, algorithms, as well as devices in the area of light and colors, shading and lighting, realistic and photorealistic imaging, definition of graphical scenes or objects, and security based on graphical objects are presented. The book also covers graphical transformations and projections, spatial imaging, curves and surfaces, filling and texturing, image filtering, virtual reality, color imaging and graphics in the service of light-source design, and analytical methods for reflection and refraction, as well as area of visualization. Topological visualization techniques for volume multifield data and "cosmos visualization" and usage of advanced related technologies such as virtual reality and graphics-based security can also be found in this book, whether it's top-down historical reconstruction in virtual reality or new graphical password schemes containing questions-background-pattern.

Finally, I would like to express my gratitude to all the authors for their valuable contributions and professional efforts in providing such precious content.

Branislav Sobota, PhD.
Assoc. Prof. Ing.
Department of Computers and Informatics,
Faculty of Electrical Engineering and Informatics,
Technical University of Kosice,
Slovak Republic

Chapter 1

Introductory Chapter: Computer Graphics and Imaging

Branislav Sobota

1. Introduction

Computer graphics is one of the generational changes in computer technology. Its development is so stormy that it has expanded from precious devices designed for military and top industrial applications to schools and households as a common information medium and a medium of education and entertainment. The history of modern computer graphics began to be written after the Second World War. Thenceforth, the area characterized as an area of technical and natural sciences dealing with the graphical information processing using a computer was named computer graphics. The graphical information is much more intelligible and clear for human than, for example, information in numerical form. A computer graphics affects our daily live. Computer graphics helped to mass-expand computers, and it removed the barriers that ordinary people feel when working with them [1] (they are "flooded" with columns of numbers and text and they are drawn into a world where they cannot be orientated oneself).

As can be seen from the previous words, human evolution is tied to the process of collecting, processing, transferring, and recording of information. If we add that most people are gaining the most information by sight, then modern computers are already greatly helping them.

However, the history of computer graphics dates back much earlier. Already Johannes Gutenberg discovered and introduced the basic technology of human information transfer—letterpress, in the years 1444–1448. Genius Leonardo da Vinci examined relationships of science and art around the same period (1452–1515). Joseph Marie Jacquard introduced a loom controlled by punch cards ("a printer predecessor?") in the years 1805–1808. But W. B. Hales created the first analog computer drawings in the years 1944–1945. Ivan Moscovich designed a drawing machine in 1951. A year later, Ben F. Laposky exposed analog computer graphics in Cherokee Sanford Museum in the USA. Then more and more attention was paid to computer graphics, and the result is already well known in present.

Yes, this is the evolution of the computer graphics phenomenon. The phenomena that are increasingly gaining interest in the eyes of the lay public are the following:

- Communication form with computers and user interfaces? Computer graphics
- Design of cars and consumer electronic products? Computer graphics
- Design of buildings and interiors? Computer graphics
- Newspapers, magazines, and catalogs? Computer graphics

- Weather forecast? Computer graphics
- Computer games and entertainment? Computer graphics
- Presentation of an economic, electoral, or statistical results? Computer graphics
- Goods packages in the shops? Computer graphics
- Film, video, and advertisement? Computer graphics
- ... and plenty other examples ...

Yes, the impact of computer graphics on our lives is really significant. It is already very difficult to find an area in which the use of computer graphics would be no importance in present. It is important not only for processing, for example, images or drawings, but also because for the graphical user interface usage. Here are some trends in computer graphics usage:

- Computer games
- Business and management graphics or advertisement
- Computer-aided drawing and design
- Visual simulation and scientific result visualization
- Image processing and cryptography
- Multimedia, show business, photorealism, user interfaces, or virtual reality and its technologies

These are trends and especially application areas of computer graphics and image processing. Computer graphics is a tool in these cases. Of course, computer graphics is also the subject of research or study.

Approximately 80% of the information is gained by sight. This has been already mentioned above. Therefore, light and colors in the process of visualization (and thus also in computer graphics) play a dominant role [2]. This dominant attribute is also used to process images or to work with graphics. From a physical point of view, light is understood as two things:

- *Particles* (photons)
- *Waves*

In this case, it is electromagnetic waves in the 10^8 Hz range. From the point of view of color, each color corresponds to a certain frequency. The range of colors ranges from red (3.8×10^8 Hz, beyond the visible spectrum continues to infrared) to purple (7.8×10^8 Hz, going beyond the visible spectrum to ultraviolet). Within the visible spectrum, a person is able to distinguish more than 4×10^5 different colors and their shades. According to the frequency transmitted by the light source, the light can be divided into:

- *Achromatic* light—this light is also called white light and contains all colors (a typical source is the sun). The combination of frequencies reflected by the body creates essentially a body color. If the frequency prevails over a certain spectrum, we are talking about the dominant frequency.

- *Monochrome* light—this light is of only one color (e.g., red).

Light is characterized by several of its attributes:

- *Color*—the basic attribute of light depends on the already mentioned frequency (or wavelength).
- *Brightness*—in fact, the intensity of light and the brightness of the light source are in direct proportion to the intensity.
- *Saturation*—saturation of color indicates its purity; the higher the saturation, the narrower the spectrum of frequencies contained in the light.
- *Lightness*—this is actually the size of the achromatic component in the light with a certain dominant frequency.

An important factor is the split of colors. There is a question as to whether there are certain basic colors, by the composition of which all others would be created. There are, however, complementary colors combined with white light. For multiple colors, a standard was created in the form of the chromatic diagram. However, the chromatic diagram does not determine which base colors the others will be composed of or their ratio. Also some chapters in this book contain description of some light and color areas with the impact to/from modern computer graphics.

Historically, computer graphics devoted much to transformations. Yes, a geometric transformation, an imaging and morphing of models or objects, is one of the most common tasks of computer graphics systems [3]. In order to manipulate with graphical objects in computer graphics, it is necessary first to define the manipulation space. Its basic property is its dimension. This dimension can be numeric or non-numeric. There are several numerical dimensions in terms of their character: topological dimension, Hausdorff (fractal) dimension, self-similarity dimension, capacity dimension, and also non-numerical dimensions, for example, information dimension, etc. All definitions of these dimensions are relative. The most used dimension is the topological dimension expressed in integer terms. The topological dimension is the range of objects commonly used in the math. Thus, the topological dimension can be also understood intuitively. With regard to the topological dimension, the most commonly used objects are:

- Zero-dimensional object (a point)
- One-dimensional object (a line, a curve)
- Two-dimensional object (an area, a surface)
- Three-dimensional object (a solid, a body)

All geometric objects convertible by continuous transformation to the above objects have the same topological dimension (e.g., a curve is assigned to a line, a plane is assigned to a surface, etc.). Typically processed objects are divided into vector and raster [1]. However, in order for the transformations to be made, it is necessary to define certain coordinate systems in respect of which the transformations are carried out. The transformations used in computer graphics are used for geometrical transformations. In the case of projections, the perspective projection is the most common. Other approaches are the axonometric projection and combinations of different projections and views. A more recent method is a 3D object morphing transformation in terms of control elements of modeling means. In terms of simulation, it is either morphing an object in a time continuum (e.g., an aging, a disintegration, etc.) or morphing an object after an interaction (a collision). In general, both defining and modeling, as well as subsequent transformations or object projections, are among the basic processes applied in computer graphics. In these cases, the curves and surfaces are often used also for graphical object definition or modeling. But the curves and surfaces are used in the computer graphics area, in particular, for two reasons. The first one, mentioned above, is their usage in the area of graphical object modeling. The second reason, nowadays, with a rising trend, is to use them "in the background" as the control attributes of various activities used in the computer graphics.

Each curve or surface must have its mathematical description for a possibility to perform various transformations with a curve/surface, such as shifts, rotations, or scale changes [3]. They are also used for 3D scanning post-processing. Here you can use these curves/surfaces designed in different shapes but with one big plus. This represents the knowledge of the mathematical notation (equations) of a curve or surface. Thus, it is possible, for example, to easily calculate the length of curve and surface area or simply shape it. Overall, it is not necessary to work with all curve/surface points but only with some curve/surface control points. The nonuniform rational B-spline (NURBS) curves/surfaces are the most flexible and also most applicable. Some curves and surfaces are usable also in some cases of special type of displaying.

It is also possible to use 3D displays instead of 2D ones (the examples of 3D displays are volumetric and holographic displays). Then a visualization and visibility solution are no longer needed. These types of displays are still relatively low-robust and low-performance devices at a very high cost. However, this does not mean that their usage is irrelevant in the future.

The performance of current computing systems allows the real-time displaying of spatial objects [4]. The results from this area are already widely used in architecture, engineering, and film (movie) industry. Displaying spatial objects began to develop with the development of the first graphical display units. Initially, it was the display of simple wire-frame models. Next, the surface of the body itself was displayed, but it was only a matter of filling the object surface with one color or simple shading. In addition, the algorithms have been developed to allow photorealistic imaging of spatial objects, allowing the display of shadows and reflections on object surfaces. But even so, it was only a piece of information about a three-dimensional space that did not allow or in part to gain spatial information from a given output. The solution, though it seems to be only partial, is to explore and exploit the very way in which human receives visual information and thus an examination and an exploitation of spatial vision.

Stereoscopic imaging is between 2D and 3D displaying but bringing to a viewer a sense of depth or space [5]. Stereoscopic vision is one of the basic characteristics and abilities of people, as well as many other forms of life on Earth. The stereoscopic projection is based on the principle of displaying different images into each eye through a special device such as glasses with different colored glasses (anaglyph), switchable glasses, polarizing glasses, stereoscopes, or helmets/glasses for virtual reality (also with mobile devices usage). For example, a color space image can be seen by an observer through switchable glasses. On the displaying device, the image for the left and the right eye is alternately displayed, and the right and the left eye are obscured in sync for the observer. The color space image can be seen also by the observer through the polarizing glasses. Both the left and right eye images are simultaneously displayed on the displaying device, but they are polarized in perpendicular planes. Overall, the perceived depth of the image is an important part of modern type displaying, for example, in virtual reality systems.

The development of new technologies within computer systems and within modern computer graphics too is taking on a dizzying pace. One of the areas where progress is most noticeable on a daily basis is undeniably virtual reality (next VR) and its related technologies [6]. VR uses computer graphics in a wide range. A virtual reality system is an interactive computer system that is capable of creating an illusion of physical presence in an imaginary or near-real world, synthesized by the VR system. A VR system provides a perfect simulation in a tightly-bound human-computer interaction environment. Thanks to the technological advances and decreasing prices, various VR devices are becoming more common in research, industry and entertainment. These are, in terms of mass interest, resulting of financial returns, a long-term "draft horse" of technological advances in associated technologies including computer graphics. Despite the indisputable advantages that the modern solutions of the VR provide, it is not a common practice to use them within a professional environment. Primary, systems based on classic user inputs and outputs such as a keyboard, a mouse, and a conventional 2D monitor continue to dominate. Although interfaces are an important feature of VR systems, they are not only the one and at all not main. The ability to create an illusion of physical presence in synthesized space, or to influence the real space with synthetic elements, can be considered dominant. The first imagination of the perfect VR was presented in the cult movie "The Matrix" and its continuations. What is real and what is virtual? VR systems provide a better experience, and they are more interactive, but the complexity of their implementation is very high. VR subsystems are divided according to senses that affect visualization subsystem, acoustic subsystem, kinetic and statokinetic subsystem, touch and contact subsystem, and other senses (e.g., smell, taste, pheromone sensitivity, etc.). Some senses commonly perceived in the real world do not have much importance to implement in the virtual world at present. However,

Figure 1.
Virtual cave in laboratory LIRKIS at technical University of Košice and the examples of immersive visualization in this environment.

the visualization subsystem is the most important, and so computer graphics is at the first place in this case. Visual immersion is very important. The virtual cave [7] in the LIRKIS laboratory at the Technical University in Košice and the examples of immersive visualizations within this cave are shown in **Figure 1**.

The abovementioned areas of computer graphics are just some of the wide range of current computer graphics. The overview of modern approaches, procedures, algorithms, as well as devices in the area of definition of graphical scenes and objects, light and colors, graphical transformations and graphical libraries and systems, projections, curves and surfaces used in computer graphics, visibility solving, filling and texturing, shading and lighting, realistic and photorealistic imaging, stereoscopy and spatial imaging, image filtering or user interfaces, and virtual reality should be the content of this book.

Author details

Branislav Sobota
Technical University of Košice, Slovakia

*Address all correspondence to: branislav.sobota@tuke.sk

References

[1] Foley J, et al. Computer Graphics—Principles and Practice, corr. sec. edit. Reading, Massachusetts: Addison-Wesley; 1997. rep 2006. p. 545. ISBN: 978-0-201-60921-9

[2] Gonzales RC, Wintz P. Digital Image Processing. 2nd ed. Reading, Massachusetts: Addison-Wesley; 1987. p. 503. ISBN: 978-0201110265

[3] Shirley P, Marschner S. Fundamentals of Computer Graphics. 3rd ed. USA: A K Peters Ltd.; 2009. p. 745. ISBN: 978-1-56881-469-8

[4] Akenine-Möller T, Haines E, Hoffman N. Real-Time Rendering. 4th ed. A K Peters/CRC Press; 2018. p. 1198. ISBN: 978-1138627000

[5] Kuszter V, Brunnett G, Pietschmann D. Exploring stereoscopic multi-user interaction with individual views. In: 2014 International Conference on Cyberworlds (CW). IEEE; 2014. pp. 101-106

[6] Korečko Š, Hudák M, Sobota B. LIRKIS CAVE: Architecture, Performance and Applications. In: Acta Polytechnica Hungarica: An International Peer-Reviewed Scientific Journal of Óbuda University, Hungarian Academy of Engineering and IEEE Hungary Section: Journal of Applied Sciences. Budapest Óbuda University. 2019;**16**(2):199-218. ISSN 1785-8860

[7] Hudák M, Korečko Š, Sobota B. Special input devices integration to LIRKIS CAVE. In: Open Computer Science. 2018;**8**(1):1-9. ISSN: 2299-1093

Chapter 2

Color Graphics in the Service of Light-Source Visualization and Design

Lulu Wang and Andrew N. Chalmers

Abstract

In the world of lighting engineering, one of the most active areas of research and industrial application is in the definition of the color rendering properties of light sources. There is a current international standard, and several new methods have been proposed over the last decade. Ordinary consumers are frequently left with little or no knowledge of how to interpret the numerical data produced by any of these systems. This situation has been exacerbated with the advent of LED light sources with widely differing properties. Certain LEDs yield very different results depending on the particular metric in use. We have designed a color graphical system that allows a user to pick a set of (typically) 16 surface color samples, and to be given a realistic comparison of the colors when illuminated by two different light sources, shown on a side-by-side display on a color monitor. This provides a visual analogy to the computations built into the above-mentioned metrics, all of which are based on comparison techniques. This chapter will provide an insight into the design and operation of our lighting computer graphics visualization system. Mention will also be made of similar systems that may be found in the published literature.

Keywords: color rendering, light sources, color graphics, comparison display, user education

1. Introduction

The purpose of the design is to display of a set of surface color patches as if they were illuminated by a specific light source, with the simultaneous display of two such sets to demonstrate the surface color differences arising from two different light sources. The approach was to implement a combination of computer graphics and image processing to generate displays providing the visualization of the color rendering properties of a range of different light sources, and to facilitate comparisons between light sources, both existing and conceptual.

Color rendering has been defined by the *Commission Internationale de l'Eclairage*: International Commission on Illumination (CIE) as the "effect of an illuminant on the perceived color of objects by conscious or subconscious comparison with their perceived color under a reference illuminant" [1]. The necessity for a means of defining the color rendering of light sources derives from the fact that human color vision possesses the property of metamerism. This can be defined as a perceived matching, for a given observer, of the colors of light sources having different (*i.e.* nonmatching) spectral power distributions [2]. In turn, an SPD (spectral power distribution) is the concentration, as a function of wavelength, of the radiant output in terms of radiant power or flux. For calculation purposes, the "given observer" is conventionally taken to be one of the standard observers as defined by the CIE [3].

In practice, what this means is that two light sources can look the same to a human observer while having different SPDs—which in turn will mean different color rendering properties. The color of the source itself is most often defined by the color temperature or correlated color temperature (CCT) [4] which will be defined and expanded on in Section 2. **Figure 1** shows two clearly different SPDs which have the same CCT.

For about the last 15 years there have been three different systems in use that provide a numerical index purporting to represent the color rendering performance of a source. The CIE color rendering index (CRI, symbol R_a) was developed in the 1960s, with some relatively minor revisions since. At the time of writing, it is still the internationally-accepted metric [6]. The color quality scale (CQS, symbol Q_a) was published by NIST [7] in 2010 with the intention of updating and improving on the calculation techniques of the CRI. Most recently, the IES of North America has published its color fidelity index (symbol R_f) in its technical memorandum TM-30-15 [8] with further improvements to the computational methods. Section 2 provides a brief outline of the above-mentioned systems used in the classification of source color properties.

It will be apparent from the foregoing that a means for the visualization of the color properties of a source will be of definite benefit to all users—particularly those concerned with light-source development, as well as users with less grasp of the physical significance of the numerical indices in the above systems. This leads us to the central focus of this chapter, which is the design and implementation of a computer graphic system providing an accurate (*i.e.* visually realistic) display of selected surface colors when illuminated (separately) by any specified pair of light sources.

Our VIS (virtual imaging system) has been developed to display the color properties of a series of test color samples under different light sources. This chapter will briefly describe the design and construction of the computer-based model that can

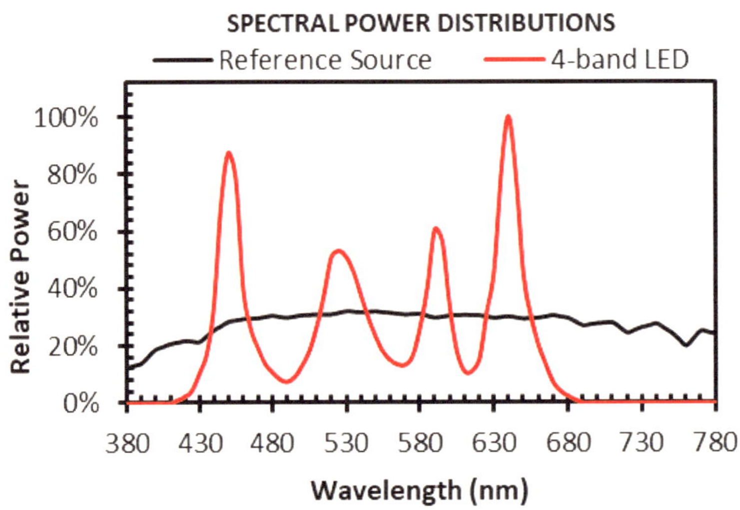

Figure 1.
Comparison of two SPDs having the same CCT: The reference source (black line) is a phase of daylight having a CCT of 5200 K shown for comparison with a 4-band LED source of the same CCT [5].

be used as a research tool for the simulation and demonstration of the color rendering properties of various artificial light sources. It will focus on the display of a set of surface color patches as if they were illuminated by a specific light source, and the simultaneous display of two such sets to demonstrate the surface color differences arising from the use of the two different light sources.

We note that modern applications for computer graphics are largely to be found in virtual reality products such as computer gaming. In these, the 3-dimensional representation of light flow, shadows, and surface highlights are critically important for the photo-realistic creation of virtual environments, and a full description of each surface's properties requires the use of concepts such as BRDF (the bidirectional reflectance distribution function). This is not the case in our VIS in which we operate on the colors of surfaces with the implied assumption of perfectly-diffusing (Lambertian) surface properties. For each surface color in our system the diffuse reflectance is represented simply by a table of values of the spectral reflectance (i.e. reflectance as a function of wavelength).

We describe the computer models developed for the representation and display of surface colors in general, and color rendering in particular. The designed system computes and displays the color of each sample from knowledge of the light-source spectrum and the spectral reflectance of each surface. It can simultaneously display the colors resulting from illumination by two different sources. In addition, the system computes the color appearance attributes for the two sets of colors using the CIECAM02 color appearance model [9].

Full details of this visualization system will be given in Section 3.

2. Color properties of light sources

2.1 The correlated color temperature

The color temperature of a light source is measured and expressed by the chromaticity coordinates (x, y) or (u, v) or (u′, v′) for that source.[1] The color of "white light" sources can also be expressed in terms of the correlated color temperature (CCT) having the unit Kevin (K). The CCT of a test source is defined as the temperature of the black body (or, Planckian) radiator having a source color that matches (as closely as possible) the color of the test source [4].

Correlated color temperature (CCT) is a widely used term to identify the appearance of near-white light sources (as well as screen white on computer monitors). It is usually the first color parameter specified in lighting system design since the color of the source has a profound influence on the atmosphere created by the lighting. The CCTs for modern lighting systems are generally in the range 2700 K (correlating with traditional tungsten filament lamps) to 6500 K (which is the color of full midday daylight in summer). Most domestic users prefer "warm" lighting in the 2700–3000 K range, while educational and commercial installations more commonly use the "cooler" range, 4000–6500 K. Note that "warm" and "cool" here refer to the psychological ambience of the lighting in contradistinction to the values of CCT.

Technically, the CCT is defined by plotting the color of the source on a CIE (u, v) graph[2] to determine the closest point on the Planckian locus, and the value of the temperature at that point gives the CCT.

[1] These sets of coordinates are all defined by the CIE and are linearly related [4].

[2] This has now been re-designated by CIE as (u′, ⅔v′).

2.2 Color rendering and fidelity

Coming now to color rendering, the three previously-mentioned systems (represented by the indices *Ra*, *Qa*, and *Rf* respectively) have a number of elements in common as well as their own distinct features. Their most important common feature is that they all produce scales in which the maximum is 100 for the "best" sources. The *Ra* scale is open-ended at its lower end, and can run to negative values, whereas the other scales terminate at zero. The *Ra* scale was originally designed to provide a measure of the relative merits of the fluorescent-tube sources being widely adopted in the 1960s; and the other two scales have been normalized in the sense that they have been scaled to provide the same index values for the original set of fluorescents. The two later scales do, however, diverge considerably from *Ra* in assessing other newer sources, particularly LEDs.

The next main factor they share is that they are all based on the comparison of sets of test colors which are illuminated in turn by a test light source and a reference source of the same CCT. In all three cases the reference sources are chosen as Planckian radiators if the CCT < 5000 K or a CIE Daylight illuminant if CCT ≥ 5000 K. Note, however, that there is a modification in the case of the TM-30-15 (*Rf*) system, in which there is a graded transition between the two types of reference for the range 4500–5500 K. In all these systems, the color differences are computed in (different) designated three-dimensional color spaces.

It should be noted that, in all three approaches, the colors and color differences are computed numerically, using the measured SPDs of test sources and the defined SPDs of the reference illuminants. The various color samples are numerically defined by means of measurements of their spectral reflectances. The wavelength ranges and wavelength intervals of the SPDs and reflectances have to be compatible, most often 380–780 nm at either 5-nm or 1-nm intervals.

Another common feature is that each of these systems incorporates a chromatic adaptation transform since it is generally not possible to achieve identity of CCTs for the test and reference sources—but there are different transforms in use in each instance.

Figure 2 summarizes the above features, showing the general format of the algorithm for a color rendering or fidelity metric. We next look at the specifics of the individual systems.

2.3 The CIE 13.3-1995 (CRI) method

In this system [6] the color rendering index (CRI) is based on the average color-difference of eight medium-chroma color samples, calculated in the (now deprecated) CIE 1964 U*V*W* color space. In order to increase the information available to users, an additional six color samples were defined, including four highly chromatic red, yellow, green and blue samples, plus colors representing foliage and human skin respectively. **Table 1** gives the complete list of CIE test colors. It also shows two synthetic grays that we added for display purposes.

After accounting for chromatic adaptation with a Von Kries correction [10], the difference in color ΔEi for each sample is calculated and used in the definition of that color's "Special CRI" as:

$$Ri = 100 - 4.6\Delta Ei \tag{1}$$

and the General CRI is the average of the first eight *Ri* values:

$$R_a = 1/8\sum_1^8 R_i \tag{2}$$

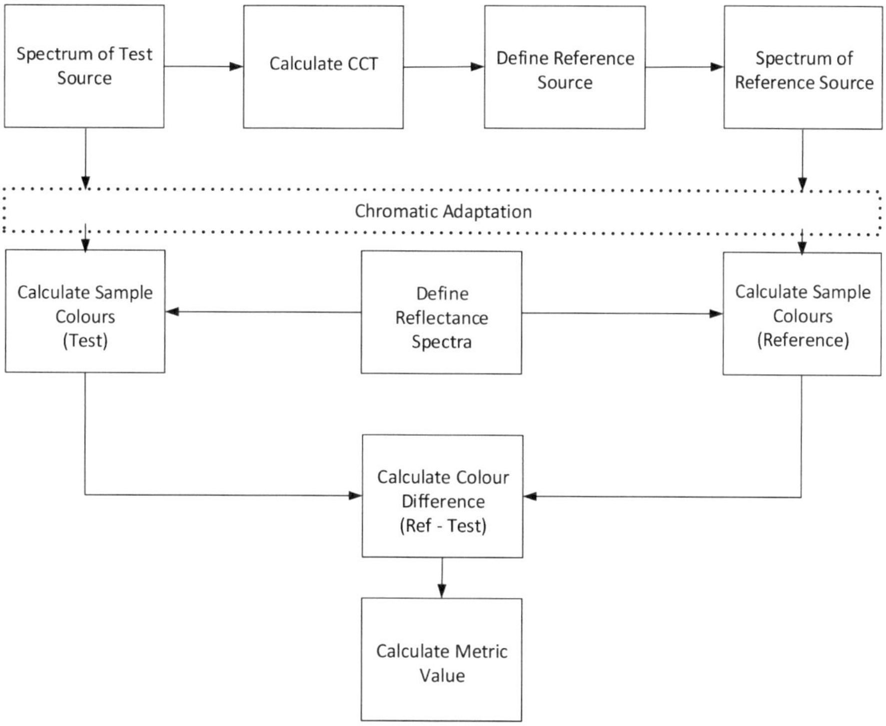

Figure 2.
General format for color rendering/fidelity metrics.

No.	Approximate Munsell notation	Color appearance under daylight
1	7.5 R 6/4	Light grayish red
2	5 Y 6/4	Dark grayish yellow
3	5 GY 6/8	Strong yellow green
4	2.5 G 6/6	Moderate yellowish green
5	10 BG 6/4	Light bluish green
6	5 PB 6/8	Light blue
7	2.5 P 6/8	Light violet
8	10 P 6/8	Light reddish purple
9	4.5 R 4/13	Strong red
10	5 Y 8/10	Strong yellow
11	4.5 G 5/8	Strong green
12	3 PB 3/11	Strong blue
13	5 YR 8/4	Light yellowish pink (light human skin)
14	5 GY 4/4	Moderate olive green (leaf green)
15	Synthetic	Dark gray
16	Synthetic	Light gray

Table 1.
CIE test color samples.

A perfect score of 100 represents zero color difference in all of the eight samples under the test source and reference illuminant. We can note here that, in today's parlance, the CIE color rendering index *Ra* is more accurately termed a color fidelity index since it gives a measure of the degree of departure from perfect agreement between the colors of surfaces under test and reference lighting conditions.

As updates on this CIE method, the two more recently-developed methods have introduced more-accurate color spaces and chromatic adaptation transforms.

2.4 The NIST (CQS) method

The following is a short summary of the main features of this method which was described in full, and contrasted with the CIE method, by Davis and Ohno in 2010 [7]. The first point of difference is in the choice of test color samples, where the CQS is based on 15 high-chroma colors selected to be representative of major significant hues. Next a new, widely-accepted chromatic adaptation transform (CMCCAT2000) [11] has been adopted. Color differences for the 15 sample colors are computed in the CIELAB (L*a*b*) (CIE 1976) color space [4].

Each color difference is then modified by a saturation factor, such that a test source that increases object chroma is not penalized. To ensure that poor rendering of any color is given sufficient weight, the differences for the 15 samples are combined by a root-mean-square “averaging” method, to give the overall color difference, ΔE_{rms}. The “rms average” score for the 15 sample colors is given by:

$$Q_{a,\,rms} = 100 - 3.1\Delta E_{rms} \tag{3}$$

In order to avoid negative index values (which may occur in *Ra* with particularly poor sources) a log-exponential conversion is used. This is further modified by a CCT factor (using a 3rd order polynomial function of CCT) which is applied to reduce the scores of sources with CCT below 3500 K. The final output is *Qa*—the color quality scale (or CQS).

This system also includes a color fidelity scale termed *Qf* which provides a metric of object color fidelity, in a similar way to *Ra* in the CIE system. *Qf* is calculated using exactly the same procedures as for *Qa*, except that it excludes the saturation factor, and the scaling factor for *Qf* in Eq. (3) is changed to 2.93.

2.5 The CIECAM02 color appearance model

A recent technical innovation is the development of the CAM02-UCS (uniform color space) [12], which is based on the CIECAM02 color appearance model [9], and is considered to be substantially better in uniformity than competitor color spaces. The CAM02-UCS also includes an improved chromatic adaptation transformation, which improves the accuracy of corrections when the comparison sources have slightly different chromaticities.

The CIECAM02 model uses a sequence of calculation steps (mostly non-linear) to derive a set of appearance attributes (lightness, chroma, and hue) that accord with human visual experience to describe the appearance of colored surfaces. The CAM02-UCS modifies the output of the process to enable the calculation of color differences that are accurate representations of perceived color difference. The details of the processes are not repeated here, and the interested reader is referred to the references [9, 12].

The proposed VIS system contains a “display CIE” button, which is able to display color appearance based on CIECAM02 model.

2.6 The IES (TM-30-15) method

Here again, we give a short overview of the new method developed, in this case, by the IES of North America [8, 13]. This method makes use of a significantly expanded range of test colors, 99 in all, representing samples from nature, human skin, textiles, paints, plastics, printed materials, and published color systems. They are termed color evaluation samples (CES) which were selected on the basis of uniformity of both color space and wavelength sampling.

The TM-30-15 method, in common with the other abovementioned methods, is based on the color differences between the test color samples under the test and reference sources, as determined in the CAM02-UCS color-difference space. These are averaged over all 99 samples, yielding the color fidelity index Rf, which has a range of 0–100, with 100 indicating an exact match with the reference, and 0 an extreme difference. In addition, the system computes a color gamut index Rg which indicates, on average, if there is an increase in color saturation ($Rg > 100$) or a decrease ($Rg < 100$).

3. Visualization system

Our virtual imaging system (VIS) is a prototype that has been designed around a Matlab® GUI. The experiments were performed using MATLAB R2015b on a computer with Intel CPU TM i7-6700 at 3.41GHz and 32GB RAM. It is a powerful research/demonstration tool allowing the user to determine and display the color properties of light sources, such as color rendering index (Ra), correlated color temperature (CCT), RGB values for the displayed color samples, and comparisons of sample color differences under different sources.

Figure 3 illustrates the basic structure, and **Figure 4** shows the complete computer modeling and display system which includes the following features:

1. A spectral measurement system to measure SPDs (spectral power distributions) of light sources and spectral reflectances of surface color samples. In many instances such data can also be obtained from published tables of SPDs and reflectances.

2. A color-managed computer display system that incorporates the following design features:

    a. Creation and display of the required virtual images by running the Matlab® GUI.

    b. A color management system incorporating monitor calibration and display control.

    c. A color-appearance computation model, based on the CIECAM02 color appearance model.

3.1 Color display model

Figure 4 represents the color computation and display model. The color management process is described in steps 2–6 below:

1. Calculation of the CIE tristimulus values [X, Y, Z] from a knowledge of the light source spectrum and the reflectance spectrum of the surface color sample, as shown in Eq. (4).

2. Measurement of monitor properties—specifically the primaries and the white point setting (usually a nominal 6500 K).

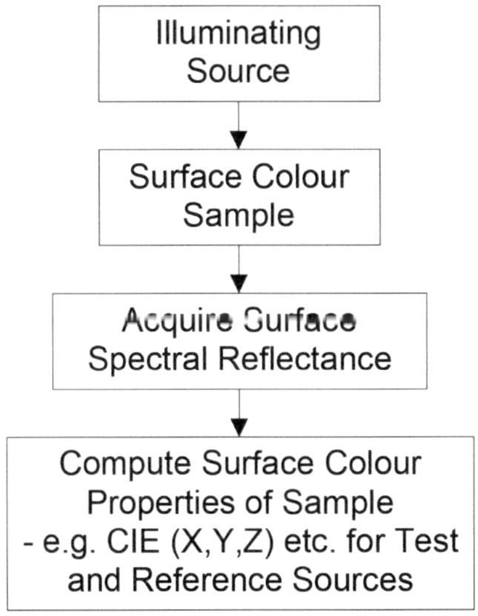

Figure 3.
Surface color model.

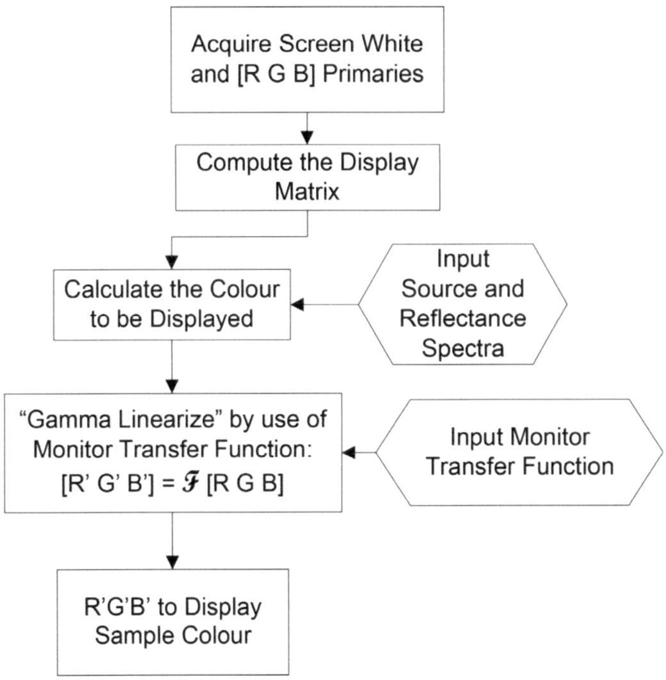

Figure 4.
Color management and display process.

3. Computing the elements mi,j (see Eq. (5)) for the monitor's display matrix by using the data from step 2.

4. Computing the [R, G, B] values for a selected color sample under a specific source from the corresponding CIE [X, Y, Z] values as shown in Eq. (5).

5. Application of the GOG model to transform the [R, G, B] values to screen [R′, G′, B′], as shown in Eq. (6).

6. Calculation of the Matlab display RGB values [SR, SG, SB] from screen [R′, G′, B′].

Note that, when the calibration steps included in this procedure are unavailable, it is still possible to obtain a useful display on any suitable monitor by the judicious use of the controls for gain (K1) and gamma that are part of the display GUI.

$$\begin{aligned} X &= \sum_{380}^{780\,nm} \bar{x}_{\lambda}.\rho_{\lambda}.\Phi_{\lambda}.\Delta\lambda \\ Y &= \sum_{380}^{780\,nm} \bar{y}_{\lambda}.\rho_{\lambda}.\Phi_{\lambda}.\Delta\lambda \\ Z &= \sum_{380}^{780\,nm} \bar{z}_{\lambda}.\rho_{\lambda}.\Phi_{\lambda}.\Delta\lambda \end{aligned} \tag{4}$$

where $\bar{x}_{\lambda}, \bar{y}_{\lambda}, \bar{z}_{\lambda}$ are the CIE 1931 color matching functions, Φ_{λ} = SPD of selected light source, $\Delta\lambda$ = wavelength interval (usually 5 nm).

$$\begin{bmatrix} R \\ G \\ B \end{bmatrix} = \begin{bmatrix} m_{11} & m_{12} & m_{13} \\ m_{21} & m_{22} & m_{23} \\ m_{31} & m_{32} & m_{33} \end{bmatrix} \begin{bmatrix} X \\ Y \\ Z \end{bmatrix} \tag{5}$$

$$L_n = (K_1 D_n + K_2)^{\gamma} \tag{6}$$

where L_n = normalized luminance of screen primary (representation of each of the quantities [R′, G′, B′] shown in **Figure 4**), D_n = normalized digital pixel value, γ = monitor gamma, K_1 = monitor gain factor, K_2 = monitor offset, and $K_1 + K_2 = 1$.

3.2 Selection of colors for display

The present VIS is a prototype that was designed around the CIE *Ra* (CRI) system. It compares a selected set of surface colors, shown under any two light sources, selected from an expandable light-source data-base. This at present comprises about 50 different sources, including 6 CIE standard illuminants. The sources may be selected to be related (i.e. having similar CCT) or unrelated, at the users' choice.

Figure 5 illustrates the operation of the system displaying 16 colors on each virtual color chart. The 16 test colors shown here are the 14 CIE test colors [6] listed in **Table 1**, with the addition of two synthetic neutral gray colors (outlined in red in **Figure 5**). In this image, the left half-screen simulates their appearance under tungsten filament (illuminant A) lighting, and the right half is under D65 daylight.

The spectral reflectances of the test colors are given in the wavelength range 380–780 nm. **Figure 6** shows the use of the *Plot Reflectances* window to display the reflectances for current selection of test colors (in this case, the 14 defined by CIE).

3.3 Selection of illuminants

The existing computer model contains two light source menus, each of which gives a list of the illuminants in the data base. They are divided into the seven groups listed below (with the origins of the current examples shown in brackets):

1. CIE standard illuminants (A, C, D50, D55, D65 and D75)
2. High pressure discharge lamps (CIE Tables H1-H5)
3. Early-generation fluorescent lamps (CIE tables FL1-FL12)
4. Later-generation fluorescent lamps (CIE tables FL3.1-FL3.15)
5. New LED 1, New LED 2, New LED 3
6. Optimized 3-, 4-, 5-, 6- and 7-band LEDs (developed by the authors using published data [14])
7. Luxeon white LED sources, 3016, 4000, 4100, 5500 and 6500 K LEDs [15].

The illuminants in groups 1–4 are published by CIE [4]. The others have been digitized from their SPD graphs for the range 380–780 nm at 5 nm interval [14, 15].

The system includes a window for the display of the currently selected illuminant spectra as shown in **Figure 7**.

3.4 Monitor calibration

The majority of displays today are designed on the assumption of 24-bit color (i.e. 8 bits per color channel) and conform with the sRGB standard. This standard (also known as IEC 61966-2-1:1999) uses the ITU-R BT.709 primaries together with a display gamma of 2.2. It was developed at a time of dominance of the display market by CRTs, but makers of LCD and OLED screens have also adopted it (by applying appropriate signal-processing techniques) for the sake of uniformity in the industry.[3]

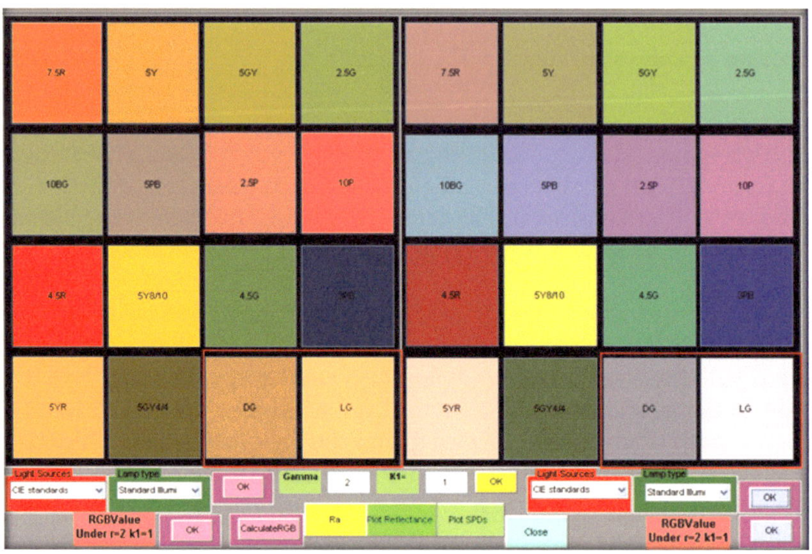

Figure 5.
Main display window of the VIS showing illuminant a (left) and D65 (right).

[3] The interested reader may wish to refer to the following commercial website that also contains a good description of the characteristics of modern monitors, and methods of measurement/calibration: http://www.displaymate.com/.

Figure 6.
Plot Reflectances window displaying the current selection of test colors. Shown here: reflectances for the 14 CIE test colors.

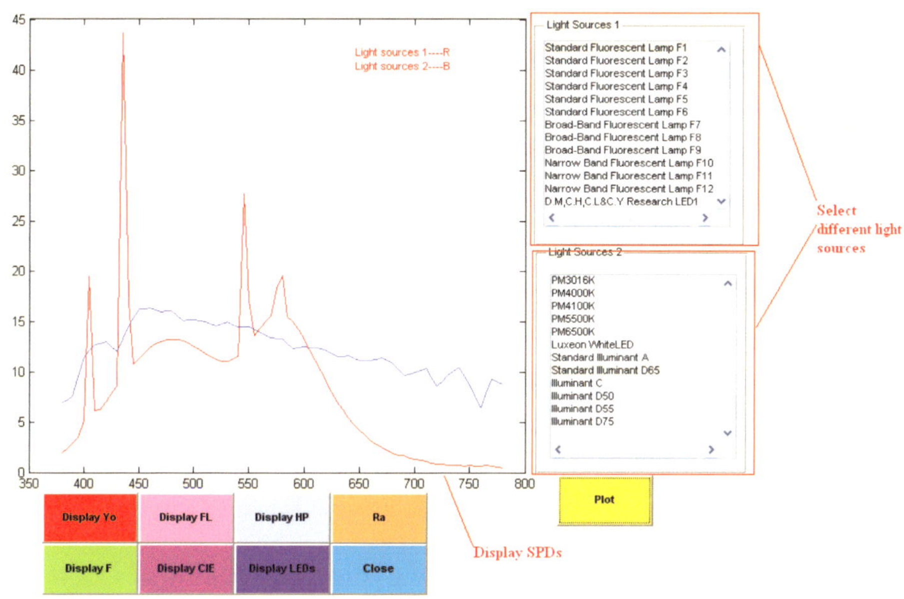

Figure 7.
Plot SPDs *window displaying current selection of illuminants. Shown here: CIE fluorescent lamp F1 6430 K (red line) and CIE daylight D65 6500 K (blue).*

The display controls in our VIS have been provided to compensate for variations that can occur in individual monitors, and will give best results with a calibrated monitor (i.e. one with known characteristics). These controls may also be used to

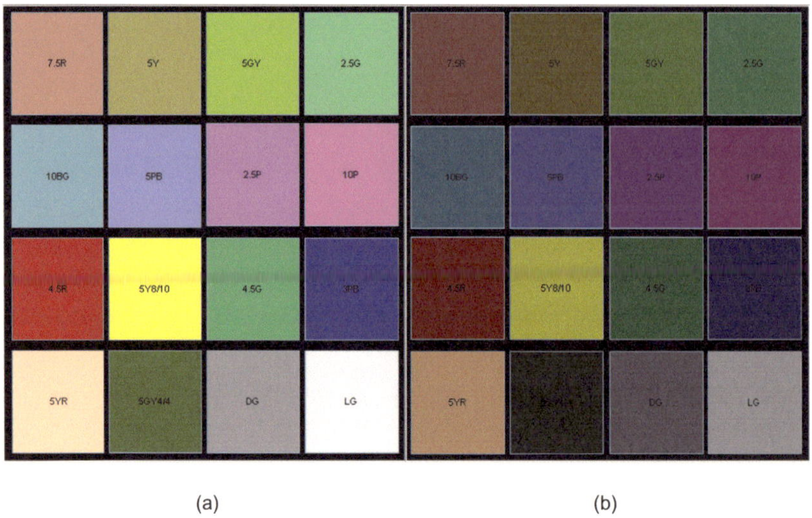

Figure 8.
Test images of CIE samples under D65 illumination, with gamma = 1.8. (a) K_1 = 1.0. (b) K_1 = 1.2.

"tweak" any uncalibrated display by following a systematic trial-and error process while displaying the 16 defined colors in both halves of the screen, and paying particular attention to the appearance of the Dark Gray and Light Gray patches.

Monitor calibration is a necessary step for the accurate rendition of the sample colors on the computer display. It was decided that this project would (at least initially) make use of CRT (cathode ray tube) monitors since there is a well-established body of literature on CRT transfer functions [16], as summarized in Eq. (6). Part of the setting-up procedure allows users to select the preferred gamma and gain (K1) values, normally close to 2.2 for gamma and 1.0 for gain. The adjustment of these settings will allow the user to optimize most modern color monitors for display purposes, but—as mentioned—calibration is required in critical applications.

Figure 8 shows two examples to illustrate the use of the display settings for user-control of the display. **Figure 8(b)** shows the effects of a bad adjustment of the controls.

4. The CIECAM02 color appearance model

One purpose of the original design was to investigate the correlation between the computed color differences and the subjectively-judged color differences as seen by a set of observers viewing the display on a calibrated monitor. For that reason, the sample colors can be computed in the CIECAM02 color appearance model, the origins and applications of which are explained in the relevant CIE technical report [9].

As seen in **Figure 4**, the system will normally be holding the [R′,G′,B′] values for each of the sample colors being displayed. In the usual operating mode, these colors are computed separately for both the test and reference sources. The opportunity therefore exists to calculate the color appearance attributes for corresponding pairs of samples (being displayed for the two different sources).

The CIECAM02 model computes the color appearance of each sample in terms of the appearance attributes [*J*, *C*, *h*] representing the lightness, chroma and hue, respectively. These are calculated from the CIE-1931 tristimulus values [X, Y, Z] by

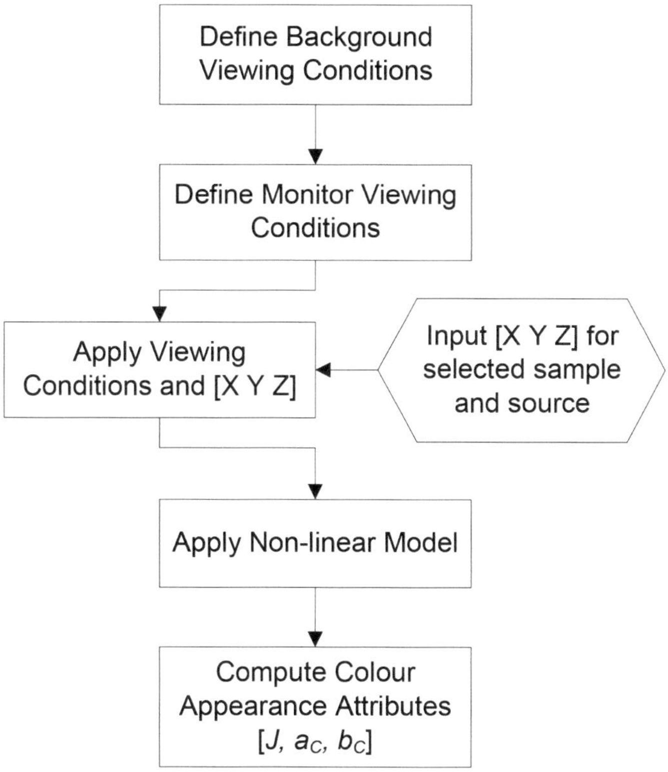

Figure 9.
Color display appearance model.

use of a somewhat complex series of non-linear transformations described in the CIE specification [9]. A number of parameters are used to model the viewing conditions experienced by the observers, as outlined below. These in turn are used to define the exact form of the non-linear relationships in the model. The procedure is outlined schematically in **Figure 9**.

In order to provide an analogy to the widely-used CIELAB (L^*, a^*, b^*) color coordinates, it is possible to define the appearance coordinates [J, a_C, b_C] using the transformations of chroma C and hue h given in Eqs. (6). Note, however, that the CIECAM02 coordinates are considered to provide a more accurate model of visual experience than the earlier CIELAB model.

$$\begin{aligned} a_C &= C.\cos(h) \\ b_C &= C.\sin(h) \end{aligned} \tag{7}$$

In using the CIECAM02 model, it is necessary to define the following viewing conditions:

- L_A—the adapting field luminance.
- Y_b—the relative luminance of the source background in the source conditions.
- c—the impact of the surround = 0.69 for average surround, or = 0.59 for dim surround.
- N_c—the chromatic induction factor = 1.0 for average surround, or = 0.9 for dim surround.

- *F*—the factor for the degree of adaptation = 1.0 for average surround, or = 0.9 for dim surround.

The CIE specification gives guidance on the assignment of numerical values to all these factors, and more detailed guidelines are available in the literature [17]. Actual luminance measurements are usually not essential; however they will assist in making the model's predictions more precise. The VIS system contains RGB function windows, which are able to get a readout of the appearance coordinates $[J, a_C, b_C]$ by use of the "display CIE" button.

5. Conclusions

A virtual imaging system has been successfully developed and prototyped, with the following outcomes.

1. A color-managed computer display system that allows the user to utilize the following design features:

    - Set up monitors for display.
    - Select light sources (from the expandable data-base of illuminants).
    - View and compare the test color images for various test light sources.

2. An SPD display system has been developed to allow the user to view the SPDs of test and reference light sources.

3. A spectral reflectance display system has been developed to allow the user to view the reflectance of each color sample.

4. Additional facilities provided:

    - Compute *Ra* and CCT of the test light source.
    - Compute the [RGB] values of each displayed color sample under different light sources.
    - Compute CIECAM02 color appearance attributes for each displayed sample.

This system can be used as a powerful tool for color rendering research, utilizing the virtual display of a set of surface colors under any pair from a range of illuminants, including older-generation light sources as well as modern high output LEDs. In addition, the designed VIS has the potential to become a useful educational tool for better understanding of color rendering among users of lighting systems and computer graphics systems.

It will also serve as a valuable educational tool to promote a better understanding of color rendering/fidelity among the users of lighting systems.

The system has been designed to facilitate the addition of new data, such as SPDs for new light sources, or additional spectral reflectances for new test colors, once the appropriate measurements are available.

Acknowledgements

The majority of the work underlying this chapter was carried out at the Institute of Biomedical Technologies of the Auckland University of Technology. The authors are indebted to the Institute's director, Professor Ahmed Al Jumaily, for making the facilities available.

This work was supported by the National Natural Science Foundation of China (Grant No. 61701159), the Natural Science Foundation of Anhui Province (Grant No. 101413246, JZ2017AKZR0129), the Fundamental Research Funds for the Central Universities (JZ2018HGTB0236), the funding from Hefei University of Technology (JZ2018HGTB0236), and the Foundation for Oversea Master Project from Ministry of Education, China (Grant No. 2160311028).

Conflict of interest

The authors declare that there is no conflict of interest regarding the publication of the content of this chapter.

Author details

Lulu Wang[1]* and Andrew N. Chalmers[2]

1 School of Instrument Science and Opto-Electronics Engineering, Hefei University of Technology, China

2 Auckland University of Technology, Auckland, New Zealand

*Address all correspondence to: luluwang2015@hfut.edu.cn

References

[1] Commission Internationale de l'Eclairage. International Lighting Vocabulary. CIE publication DIS 017/E: 2016. Vienna: CIE; 2017

[2] Wyszecki G, Stiles WS. Color Science —Concepts and Methods, Quantitative Data and Formulae. 2nd ed. New York: John Wiley & Sons; 1982. p. 184

[3] Wyszecki G, Stiles WS. Color Science —Concepts and Methods, Quantitative Data and Formulae. 2nd ed. New York: John Wiley & Sons; 1982. pp. 130-143

[4] Commission Internationale de l'Eclairage. Colorimetry. CIE Publication 15.3. 3rd ed. Vienna: CIE; 2003

[5] Illuminating Engineering Society of North America. Official Version Of Excel Worksheet, Available with Purchase of the IES TM-30-15 Technical Memorandum. 2015. Available from: http://www.ies.org/redirect/tm-30/ [Accessed: Nov 20, 2015]

[6] Commission Internationale de l'Eclairage. Method of Measuring and Specifying Colour Rendering Properties of Light Sources. CIE Publication 13.3. Vienna: CIE; 1995

[7] Davis W, Ohno Y. Color quality scale. Optical Engineering. 2010;**49**(3): 1-16. Article ID: 033602. DOI: 10.1117/1.3360335

[8] Illuminating Engineering Society of North America. IES Method for Evaluating Light Source Color Rendition. Technical Memorandum TM-30-15. New York: Illuminating Engineering Society; 2015

[9] Commission Internationale de l'Eclairage. A Colour Appearance Model for Colour Management Systems: CIECAM02. CIE Publication 159. Vienna: CIE; 2004

[10] Wyszecki G, Stiles WS. A Colour Appearance Model for Colour Management Systems: CIECAM02. CIE Publication 159. Vienna: CIE; 2004. pp. 429-432

[11] Li CJ, Luo MR, Rigg B, Hunt RWG. CMC 2000 chromatic adaptation transform: CMCCAT2000. Color Research & Application. 2002;**27**:49-58

[12] Luo MR, Cui G, Li C. Uniform colour spaces based on CIECAM02 colour appearance model. Color Research and Application. 2006;**31**: 320-330. DOI: 10.1002/col.20227

[13] U.S. Department of Energy Building Technologies Office. Solid-State Lighting Technology Fact Sheet— Evaluating Color Rendition Using IES TM-30-15. Available from: https://www.energy.gov/sites/prod/files/2015/12/f27/tm-30_fact-sheet.pdf [Accessed: Jul 3, 2018]

[14] Wang L, Chalmers AN. High-luminous efficacy light sources. In: BE Hons Mini-Conference. New Zealand: Department of Electrical & Electronic Engineering, Manukau Institute of Technology; 2007

[15] Lumileds Lighting. LUXEON® K2 Emitter. Technical Datasheet DS51, San Jose, Calif.: Lumileds Lighting US. LLC.; 2006

[16] Berns RS, Motta RJ, Gorzynski ME. CRT colorimetry. Part I: Theory and practice. Color Research and Application. 1993;**18**:299-314

[17] Moroney N, Fairchild MD, Hunt RWG, Li C, Luo MR, Newman T. The CIECAM02 Color Appearance Model. Available from: http://rit-mcsl.org/fairchild/PDFs/PRO19.pdf [Accessed: Aug 24, 2018]

Chapter 3

Analytical Method for Reflection and Refraction

Nobuhiko Mukai

Abstract

In computer graphics, ray tracing is very simple and powerful method to present physical phenomena especially light-related things such as reflection and refraction since it traces the ray from the eye to the light source; however, we cannot understand how the result image is generated. Then, this chapter describes the mechanism of reflection and refraction. It is very time-consuming to render the target object considering reflection and refraction. If the object distorted by reflection and refraction is previously obtained, it is very fast to generate the result image since all we have to do is to render the distorted object without considering reflection and refraction. In the proposed method, firstly, a virtual object, which is constructed with vertices translated from original ones by considering reflection and refraction, is generated. Then, the image with reflection and refraction is generated by rendering the virtual object. In the analysis, total reflection and attenuation of light power are also considered. At last, the proposed method is applied to two types of transparent objects: cubed glass and cylindrical glass, and the comparison between the simulation results and the real photos is performed to demonstrate that the generated images are the same as the real ones.

Keywords: reflection, refraction, virtual object, total refection, ray tracing, cubed glass, cylindrical glass

1. Introduction

Computer graphics is a very powerful tool to visualize natural phenomena such as thunder with lighting, avalanche in blizzard, reflection on a glass window, and so on. Among them, one of the most challenging issues is to visualize optical-related phenomena such as reflection and refraction. Although ray tracing is the most powerful method, it takes huge amount of time to trace the ray that has emitted from a light source and reaches the eye through each pixel of an image. The method searches the trace by dividing it to two phenomena: reflection and refraction. It generates the image with a recursive process so that the image can be generated with a simple algorithm. However, the image generated on a glass by reflection and refraction is so complicated that we cannot understand which part of the image is generated by reflection and/or refraction.

Then, this chapter describes an analytical method that draws an image generated on a geometrically defined object such as parallel glass, cubed glass, or cylindrical glass by reflection and/or refraction. The method analyzes the trace of the ray in a transparent object and generates a virtual object, which is constructed with vertices translated from original ones by considering reflection and refraction. In addition, the mechanism of total reflection and the attenuation of light power are also investigated. Thereafter, each image with reflection and/or refraction is generated by rendering the virtual object without considering reflection and refraction. Then, the final image is generated by combining every image drawn separately with the virtual objects.

Moreover, two types of applications with the proposed method are presented. One is to generate the image with reflection and refraction on a cubed glass, where there are six facets that have different number of reflection and refraction, and also total reflection happens on some facets depending on the eye position. The other is to represent a refractive image on a cylindrical glass, where four refractions happen when the light passes in the interior of the cylindrical glass.

At last, in order to demonstrate that the images generated with the proposed method are realistic, the simulation images are compared with real photos. One is the image that has reflection and refraction on a cubed glass, and the other is one that has refraction on a cylindrical glass.

2. Related works

In generation of realistic images with computer graphics, Whitted invented ray tracing [1, 2], which is the most simple and powerful method; however, it requires a lot of time to trace the ray for every pixel of the image. Then, Heckbert et al. proposed beam tracing [3] and Amanatides suggested cone tracing [4]. These methods are faster than ray tracing because they trace the ray not for each pixel but for the bundle of it by utilizing spatial coherence. On the other hand, Blinn et al. had invented texture mapping [5] to generate realistic images with a simple and fast method. Then, Pauline et al. used texture mapping to represent waves [6], and Hakura et al. proposed parameterized environment mapping [7], which is an extended method of texture mapping and reproduces local reflection from pre-rendered viewpoints. Texture mapping can create realistic images in real time since some pre-generated texture images are used in the rendering; however, multiple images must be prepared especially when the viewpoint changes. Then, G'enevaux et al. suggested another method to obtain realistic and interactive effect of refraction [8].

On the other hand, Ofek et al. had proposed a method to generate reflective images by using virtual objects that are previously transformed from the original ones [9]. Conversely, Iwasaki et al. used texture mapping to render caustics on water surfaces [10]. Wang et al. also utilized environment mapping and interpolated the map in real time by using depth buffer [11].

Nowadays, graphics processing unit (GPU) is utilized for general purpose calculation that is used to be performed by central processing unit (CPU). Then, Wyman used GPU and performed an interactive image-space approach to represent refractive images on transparent objects [12]. Hu et al. also utilized GPU power and proposed an interactive computing scheme for rendering of reflection, refraction, and caustics [13]. In addition, Oliveira et al. utilized programmable GPU for image-space technique that calculates the intersection between the ray and objects efficiently [14]. Furthermore, Rodgman et al. proposed another rendering method for refraction in volume graphics [15], and Rousiers et al. also proposed another method for representing refraction through a transparent object that has rough surfaces [16]. On the contrary, Chen et al. suggested a depth acquisition method from refractive images, which method can measure the depth from the eye if the cause of refraction is already known [17]. If we use this method, we can estimate the original shape of objects deformed by refraction.

Generating realistic images with reflection and refraction requires huge amount of time so that most of research use texture mapping with the help of GPU power. Although these techniques produce realistic images with reflection and refraction very fast, we do not understand which part of the image is generated by reflection and/or refraction. On the contrary, the virtual object that Ofek et al. [9] proposed has vertices translated from the original ones by considering reflection. Then, if we can understand how the original object is transformed by reflection and refraction, the image can be generated very fast. Therefore, Mukai et al. investigated how the vertices of an object are translated from the original ones by refraction in a cylindrical glass [18] and also represented the complex image on a cubed glass by combining each image that has simple reflection and/or refraction [19]. Therefore, this chapter describes how an object is transformed by reflection and refraction and how the vertices constructing the object are translated from the original positions. First, the analysis of reflection and refraction is described, and a virtual object, which is transformed from the original one by reflection and refraction, is generated. Then, the image with reflection and refraction is generated by combining each image rendered with the virtual object. At last, the proposed method is used for two types of applications: the image with reflection and refraction generated on a cubed glass and the image with refraction generated on a cylindrical glass. In addition, the result shows that the simulation images are the same as the real ones by comparison between the generated images and the real photos.

3. Virtual object

3.1 Reflection

This section describes how to generate a virtual object, which has vertices translated from original ones by considering reflection. **Figure 1** illustrates the

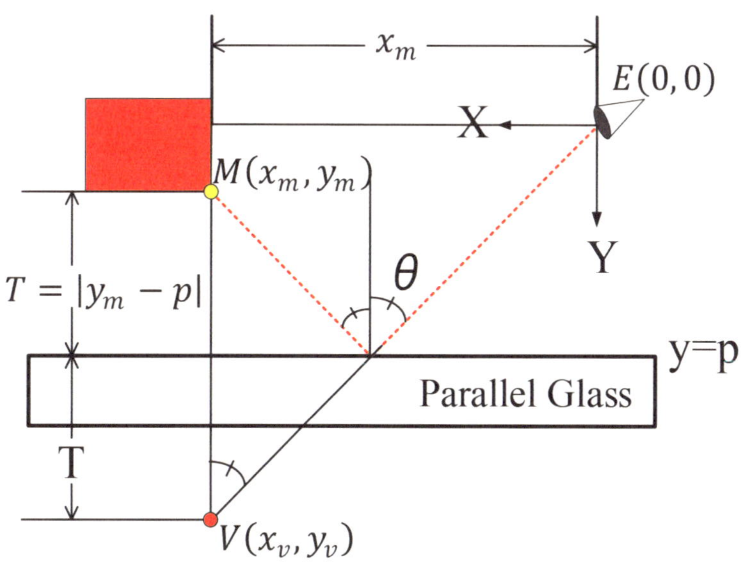

Figure 1.
Virtual vertex due to reflection on a parallel glass.

reflection on a parallel glass. In the figure, $E(0,0)$, θ, and $M(x_m, y_m)$ are the eye position that is the origin of the Cartesian coordinate system, incident angle of light on the front plane of the parallel glass, and one vertex constructing the object shown in red, respectively. The dotted red line shows the trace of the ray that has emitted from a vertex $M(x_m, y_m)$ and enters the eye position $E(0,0)$. The front plane of the parallel glass is placed on y = p. If $V(x_v, y_v)$ is obtained, we can generate the image by just rendering the virtual object including $V(x_v, y_v)$ instead of the original one including $M(x_m, y_m)$. The virtual vertex $V(x_v, y_v)$ translated from the original vertex $M(x_m, y_m)$ is calculated as follows:

$$V(x_v, y_v) = V(x_m, y_m + 2T) = V(x_m, y_m + 2p - y_m) \;(\because y_m \le p) \tag{1}$$

3.2 Refraction

Figure 2 shows the refraction through a parallel glass, which has the thickness of H. In the figure, n_1 and n_2 are the refractive indices of the air and the glass, respectively. The incidence angle of the ray that outputs from the eye is θ, and the refraction angle is ϕ. If $V(x_v, y_v)$ is obtained, we can generate the image by just rendering the virtual object with $V(x_v, y_v)$ instead of the original one with $M(x_m, y_m)$. Then, the virtual vertex $V(x_v, y_v)$ is calculated as the following:

$$L_y = \mathrm{H}\tan(\phi)\, tan\,\{(\pi/2) - \theta\} \tag{2}$$

$$\therefore L_y = \mathrm{H}\{1 - \, tan\,(\phi)\, tan\,[(\pi/2) - \theta]\} = \mathrm{H}\{1 - \, tan\,(\phi)/\, tan\,(\theta)\} \tag{3}$$

However, θ is the incidence angle for the vertex $M(x_m, y_m)$ constructing the original object, and the angle θ depends on the positions of $E(0,0)$ and $M(x_m, y_m)$. On the other hand, we can obtain the following equations from △ EOM in **Figure 2** and Snell's law:

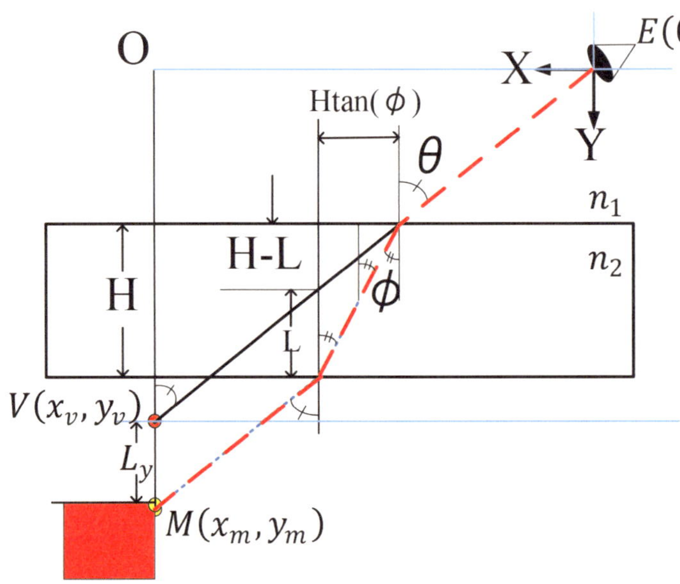

Figure 2.
Virtual vertex due to refraction through a parallel glass.

$$tan\,(\theta) = x_m/\left(y_m - L_y\right) \tag{4}$$

$$n_1 \sin\,(\theta) = n_2 \sin\,(\phi) \tag{5}$$

By substituting Eqs. (4) and (5) to Eq. (3), the following equation is obtained:

$$x_m = \left(y_m - H\right) tan\,(\theta) + \mathrm{H}\tan\left\{ sin^{-1}[(n_1/n_2)\, sin\,(\theta)]\right\} \tag{6}$$

Finally, by solving Eq. (6) with an iterative method, the incidence angle θ is calculated. With the calculated incident angle θ, ϕ is also calculated with Eq. (5). Then, the vertex of the virtual object is calculated as follows:

$$\mathrm{V}\left(x_v, y_v\right) = \mathrm{V}\left(x_m, y_m - L\right) \tag{7}$$

3.3 Inclination of a plane

The above description is true for the case that the reflective or the refractive plane is parallel to X axis of the coordinate system. However, the rotation of the coordinate system is required for the case that the plane is inclined against X axis. **Figure 3** shows the process of the vertex translation with the coordinate system rotation. In **Figure 3(a)**, the plane is inclined against X axis by the angle ω. By the rotation, the plane becomes parallel to X axis, and the translation of the vertex A in **Figure 3(b)** is performed with the above process (the translated vertex is indicated as B in the figure). Then, the final vertex is obtained by the inverse rotation of the coordinate system.

3.4 Combination of reflection and refraction

Figure 4 shows the case where both reflection and refraction happen on a parallel glass. $\mathrm{M}\left(x_m, y_m\right)$ is a vertex that constructs an original object, and D is the thickness of the parallel glass. The ray that has emitted from $\mathrm{M}\left(x_m, y_m\right)$ is refracted on the front plane of the glass and also reflected on the back plane. Then, the ray reaches the eye after it is refracted again on the front plane. If we can calculate the temporary virtual vertex for the reflection on the back plane, we can consider this phenomenon, which has two refractions and one reflection, as another phenomenon that has two refractions and no reflection with another parallel glass which thickness is $2D$ instead of D. In the figure, this temporary vertex is shown as $M_1\left(x_m, y_1\right)$. In addition, if we can calculate the virtual vertex, we can consider the

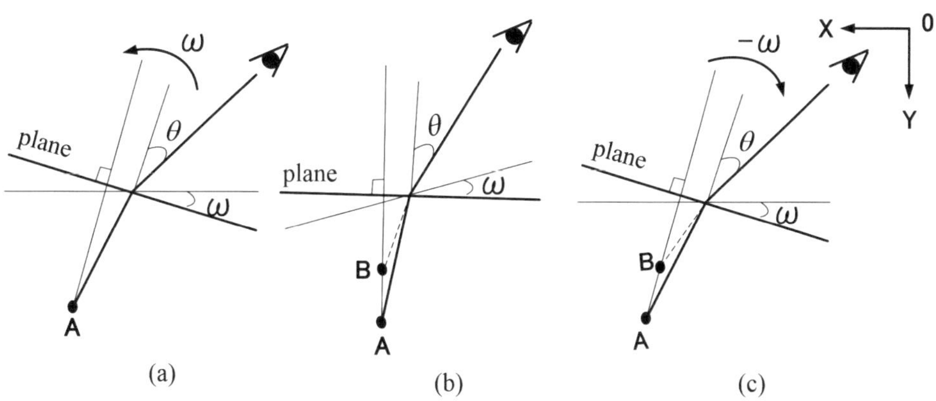

Figure 3.
Vertex translation with the coordinate system rotation. (a) Rotation (b) Movement and (c) Inverse rotation.

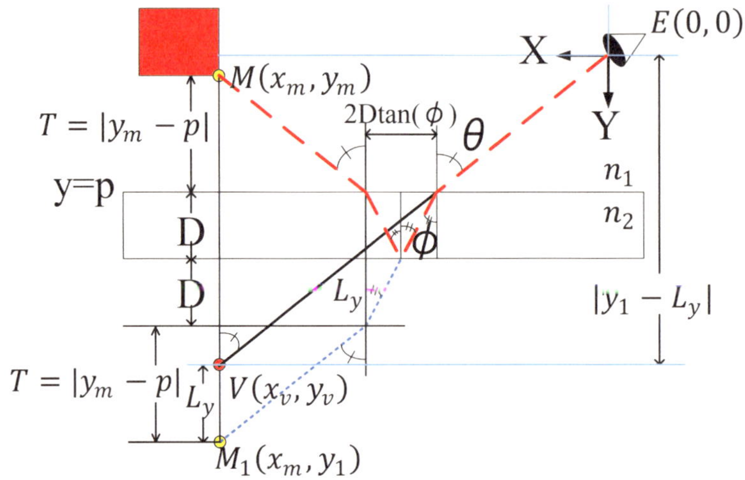

Figure 4.
Reflection and refraction on a parallel glass.

phenomenon as another phenomenon with no reflection and no refraction. This virtual vertex is shown as $V(x_v, y_v)$ in the figure. If we can obtain the virtual vertex $V(x_v, y_v)$, we can draw the image without considering both reflection and refraction. The final virtual vertex $V(x_v, y_v)$ is calculated as follows:

$$M_1(x_m, y_1) = M_1(x_m, y_m + 2\{T + D\}) = M_1(x_m, y_m + 2\{|y_m - p| + D\})$$
$$= M_1(x_m, 2p - y_m + 2D) \quad (8)$$
$$2D - L_y = 2Dtan(\phi)\, tan\,\{(\pi/2) - \theta\} = 2D\, tan\,(\phi)/\, tan\,(\theta) \quad (9)$$
$$\therefore L_y = 2D\{1 - tan\,(\phi)/\, tan\,(\theta)\} \quad (10)$$

We can also obtain the following equation from Eq. (4) by replacing y_m with y_1:

$$tan\,(\theta) = x_m/(y_1 - L_y) \quad (11)$$

By substituting Eqs. (5) and (11) for Eq.(10), the following equation is obtained:

$$x_m = (y_1 - 2D)\, tan\,(\theta) + 2Dtan\{sin^{-1}[(n_1/n_2)\, sin\,(\theta)]\} \quad (12)$$

From Eq. (8), $y_1 = 2p - y_m + 2D$. Then, Eq. (12) can be solved with an iterative method because θ varies depending on the positions of the eye and each object. If θ is decided, we can calculate the virtual vertex $V(x_v, y_v)$ as follows:

$$V(x_v, y_v) = V(x_m, 2p - y_m + 2D - L_y) = V(x_m, 2p - y_m + 2D\{tan\,(\phi)/\, tan\,(\theta)\})$$
$$(13)$$

The same calculation can be applied to the general phenomenon with $n = 2k - 1$ $(k \geq 1)$ repetitive reflections inside the parallel glass and two refractions on the front plane:

$$L_y = 2kD\{1 - tan\,(\phi)/\, tan\,(\theta)\} \quad (14)$$
$$x_m = \{y_1 - 2kD\}\, tan\,(\theta) + 2kDtan\{sin^{-1}[(n_1/n_2)\, sin\,(\theta)]\} \quad (15)$$
$$V(x_v, y_v) = V(x_m, 2p - y_m + 2kD\{tan\,(\phi)/\, tan\,(\theta)\}) \quad (16)$$

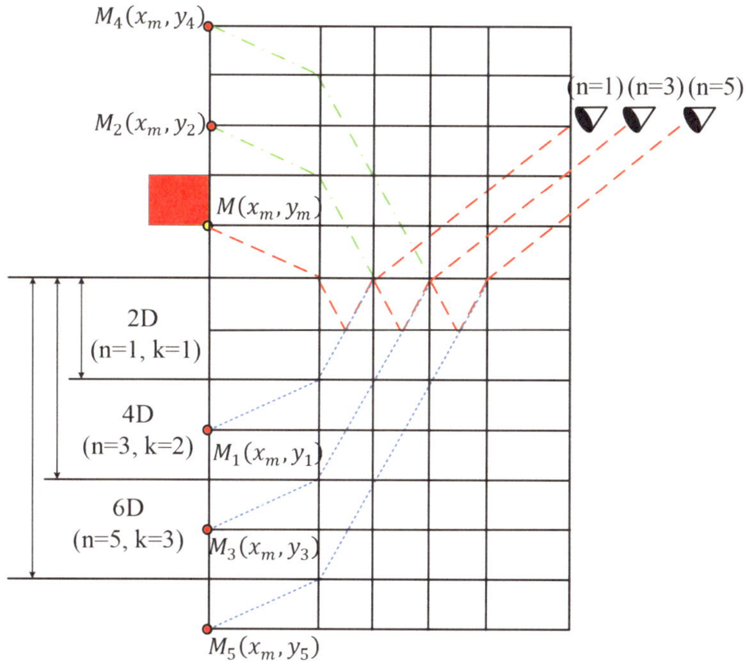

Figure 5.
Relation between the number of reflection and the thickness of the glass.

Figure 5 shows the relation between the number of repetitive reflections inside the parallel glass and the thickness of the virtual glass. The original thickness of the glass is D. When there is 1 = 2k − 1 (k = 1) reflection inside the glass, we can consider the phenomenon as another phenomenon that has no reflection inside the glass and two refractions on the side planes with the parallel glass, which thickness is 2D = 2kD (k = 1). When the number of the reflection is 3 = 2k − 1 (k = 2) or 5 = 2k − 1 (k = 3), the thickness of the glass becomes 4D = 2kD (k = 2)4D or 6D = 2kD (k = 3), respectively.

3.5 Total reflection

When light enters the side plane of the glass, the incident angle changes. If the incident angle on the back plane of the glass is over the critical angle, total reflection happens. That is, there is no refraction and all light energy is reflected on the back plane. Even in this case, we can consider the phenomenon, which has one total reflection on the back plane and two refractions on the both side planes, as another phenomenon that has only two refractions on the side planes and no reflection on the back plane. In addition, we can generate the image by rendering the virtual object that has virtual vertices. **Figure 6** illustrates this situation. In the figure, it is supposed that the back plane of the parallel glass is placed on y = q, and the incident and refractive angles on the side planes are θ and ϕ, respectively. Then, the difference of the reflective angle ψ of the back plane and the critical angle ψ_c, which is defined as $sin^{-1}(n_1/n_2)$, can be calculated as follows by using Eq. (5):

$$sin^2(\psi) - sin^2(\psi_c) = sin^2\left\{\left(\frac{\pi}{2}\right) - \phi\right\} - \left(\frac{n_1}{n_2}\right)^2 = cos^2(\phi) - \left(\frac{n_1}{n_2}\right)^2$$
$$= 1 - sin^2(\phi) - \left(\frac{n_1}{n_2}\right)^2 = 1 - \left(\frac{n_1}{n_2}\right)^2 sin^2(\theta) - \left(\frac{n_1}{n_2}\right)^2 = 1 - \left(\frac{n_1}{n_2}\right)^2 \{1 + sin^2(\theta)\} \tag{17}$$

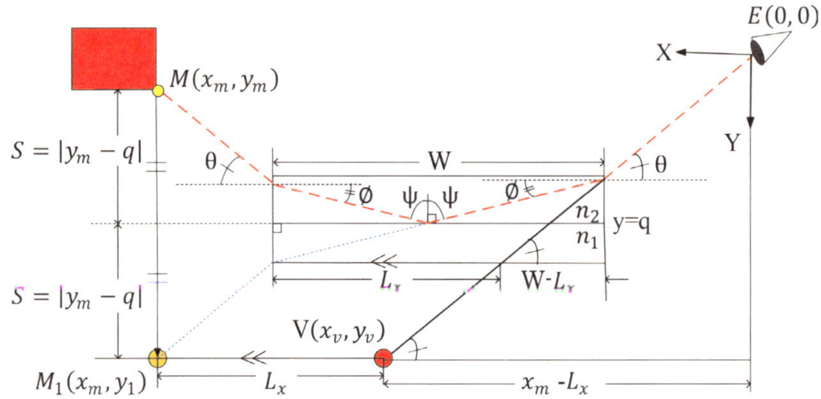

Figure 6.
Total reflection.

Here, n_1 and n_2 are the refractive indices of the air and the glass, respectively. n_1 is 1.0 and n_1 is in [1.43, 2.14] if we use the normal glass. Then, Eq. (17) is greater than 0.02 and always plus number. That means total reflection always happens on the back plane when light enters the side of the glass. Even in this case, we can consider the phenomenon, which has one total reflection on the back plane and two refractions on the both side planes of the parallel glass, as another phenomenon that has only two refractions on the side planes and no total reflection by using a virtual vertex shown as $M_1(x_m, y_1)$ in the figure. It is also supposed that the position of the back plane is y = q.

From the figure, the following equations are obtained:

$$M_1(x_m, y_1) = M_1(x_m, 2S + y_m) = M_1(x_m, 2|y_m - q| + y_m) = M(x_m, 2q - y_m) \tag{18}$$

$$(W - L_x)\tan(\theta) = W\tan(\phi) \tag{19}$$

$$\therefore L_x = W\{1 - \tan(\phi)/\tan(\theta)\} \tag{20}$$

$$\tan(\theta) = y_1/(x_m - L_x)\ (\because x_m \geq L_x) \tag{21}$$

With Eqs. (5), (20), and (21), the following equation is derived:

$$2q - y_m = (x_m - W)\tan(\theta) + W\tan\{\sin^{-1}[(n_1/n_2)\sin(\theta)]\} \tag{22}$$

Then, the incident angle θ is calculated with an iterative method, and ϕ is also calculated with Eq. (5). Finally, the virtual vertex is obtained as the following:

$$V(x_v, y_v) = V(x_m - L_x, 2q - y_m) = V(x_m - W\{1 - \tan(\phi)/\tan(\theta)\}, 2q - y_m) \tag{23}$$

Figure 7 shows the case that has two total reflections. In this case, we can consider the phenomenon, which has two total reflections on the front and back planes, and two refractions on the both sides, as another phenomenon that has one total reflection on the back plane and two refractions on the both sides by using a virtual vertex $M_1(x_m, y_1)$. In addition, we can consider the phenomenon as another phenomenon that has no total reflection and two refractions on the both sides by using another virtual vertex $M_2(x_m, y_2)$. Finally, we can consider the phenomenon as another one that has no total reflection and no refraction by using $V(x_v, y_v)$.

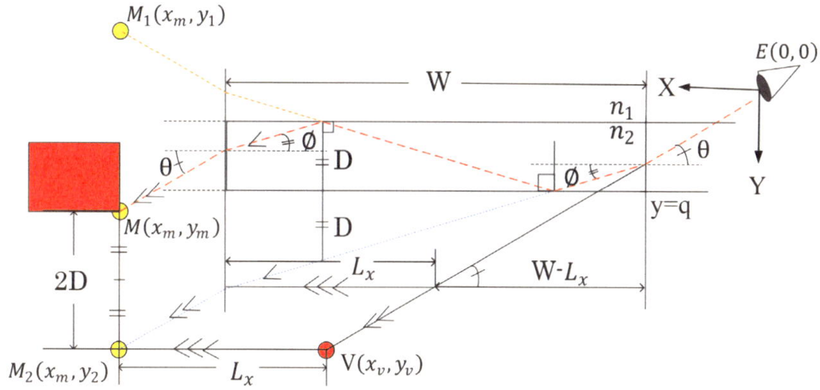

Figure 7.
Two total reflections.

$M_2(x_m, y_2)$ and $V(x_v, y_v)$ are calculated as follows by using Eq. (20):

$$M_2(x_m, y_2) = M_2(x_m, y_m + 2D) \tag{24}$$

$$V(x_v, y_v) = V(x_m - L_x, y_m + 2D) = V(x_m - W\{1 - \tan(\phi)/\tan(\theta)\}, y_m + 2D) \tag{25}$$

Figure 8 shows another case that has three total reflections. Even in this case, we can consider the phenomenon as another one that has no total reflection and two refractions on the both sides by using a virtual vertex $M_3(x_m, y_3)$. Then, we can generate the image without considering any reflection and refraction by using another virtual vertex $V(x_v, y_v)$.

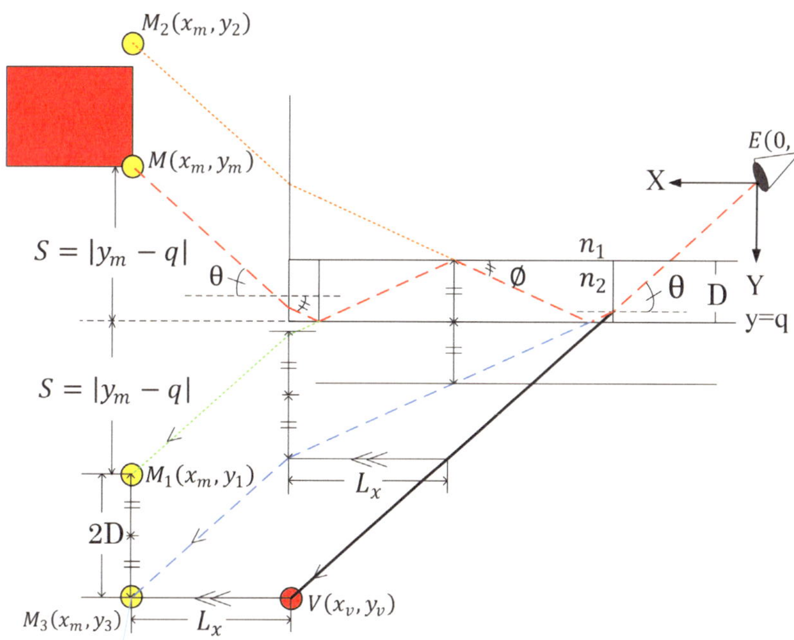

Figure 8.
Three total reflections.

$M_3(x_m, y_3)$ and $V(x_v, y_v)$ are calculated as follows by using Eq. (20):

$$M_3(x_m, y_3) = M_3(x_m, y_m + 2\{S + D\}) = M_3(x_m, y_m + 2\{|y_m - q| + D\}) \\ = M_3(x_m, 2q - y_m + 2D) \quad (26)$$

$$V(x_v, y_v) = V(x_m - L_x, 2q - y_m + 2D) \\ = V(x_m - W\{1 - \tan(\phi)/\tan(\theta)\}, 2q - y_m + 2D) \quad (27)$$

The same calculation can be applied to the case that has n total reflections inside the glass. In fact, $V(x_n, y_n)$ is classified to two types depending on the number of total reflection as the following:

$$V(x_v, y_v) = \\ \begin{cases} V(x_m - W\{1 - \tan(\phi)/\tan(\theta)\}, 2q - y_m + (n-1)D) & (n = 2k-1, k \geq 1) \\ V(x_m - W\{1 - \tan(\phi)/\tan(\theta)\}, y_m + nD) & (n = 2k, k \geq 1) \end{cases} \quad (28)$$

3.6 Attenuation

Figure 9 shows the case that has multiple reflections and refractions in the parallel glass, where light energy attenuates gradually every time reflection or refraction happens.

Fresnel equations mention that the reflection rate changes depending on the incident angle; however, the following approximated equation is usually used for the reflection rate calculation in computer graphics field:

$$F_r(\theta) = F_0 + (1 - F_0)(1 - \cos(\theta))^5 \quad (29)$$

$$F_0 = \{(n_1 - n_2)/(n_1 + n_2)\} \quad (30)$$

where θ is the incident angle and n_1 and n_2 are the refractive indices of the air and the glass, respectively. In addition, F_0 is the reflection rate in the case that light enters the plane perpendicularly. If the total energy of light is 1, the summation of the first reflective light energy (R_1) and the first transmitted light energy (T_1) should be 1. Then, the reflective and the refractive energies after n reflections and refractions can be calculated as follows if there is no energy loss:

$$R_1 = F_r(\theta) \quad (31)$$

$$T_1 = 1 - R_1 = 1 - F_r(\theta) \quad (32)$$

$$R_2 = T_1 F_r(\phi) = \{1 - F_r(\theta)\}F_r(\phi) \quad (33)$$

$$T_2 = T_1\{1 - F_r(\phi)\} = \{1 - F_r(\theta)\}\{1 - F_r(\phi)\} \quad (34)$$

$$R_3 = R_2 F_r(\phi) = \{1 - F_r(\theta)\}F_r(\phi)^2 \quad (35)$$

$$T_3 = R_2\{1 - F_r(\phi)\} = \{1 - F_r(\theta)\}F_r(\phi)\{1 - F_r(\phi)\} \quad (36)$$

$$R_n = \{1 - F_r(\theta)\}F_r(\phi)^{n-1} \ (n \geq 2) \quad (37)$$

$$T_n = \{1 - F_r(\theta)\}F_r(\phi)^{n-2}\{1 - F_r(\phi)\} \ (n \geq 2) \quad (38)$$

In the rendering, the reflection and the refraction rates are used as an alpha value for alpha blending, when multiple images are combined together.

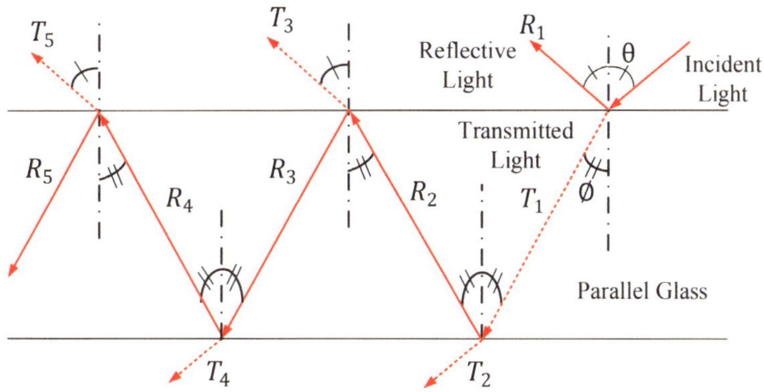

Figure 9.
Multiple reflections and refractions.

4. Cubed glass

4.1 Analysis of reflection and refraction

Figure 10 shows an image generated on a cubed glass, which image has some reflections and refractions. We can estimate that there is a string of "GRAPHICS" under the cubed glass; however, we do not know how the image is generated and which part has the effect of reflection, refraction, or the combination. We can see that the top plane is divided into four regions and some images are flipped horizontally, vertically, or on both directions. On the other hand, **Figure 11** illustrates the ray path in the cubed glass. In **Figures 10** and **11**, eight points indicated as A to H are the vertices constructing the cubed glass. In **Figure 10**, four numbers

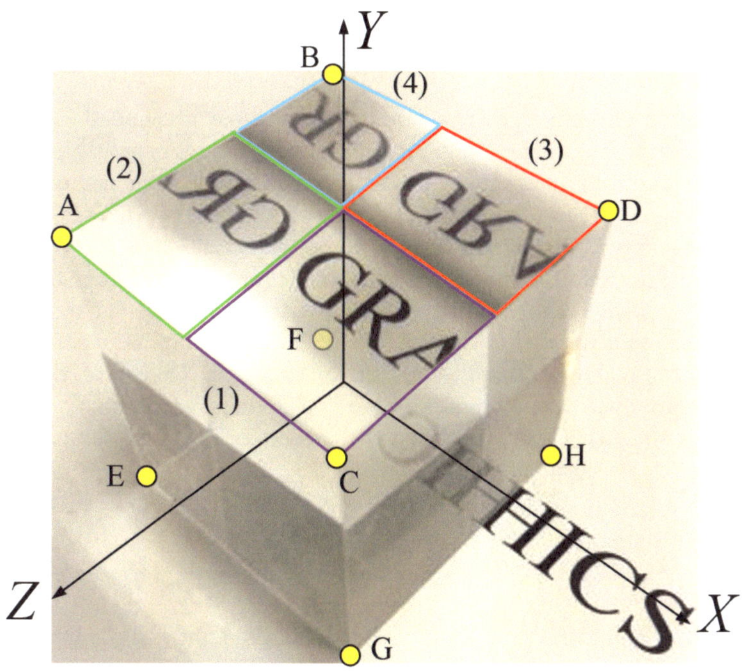

Figure 10.
Reflective and refractive image on a cubed glass.

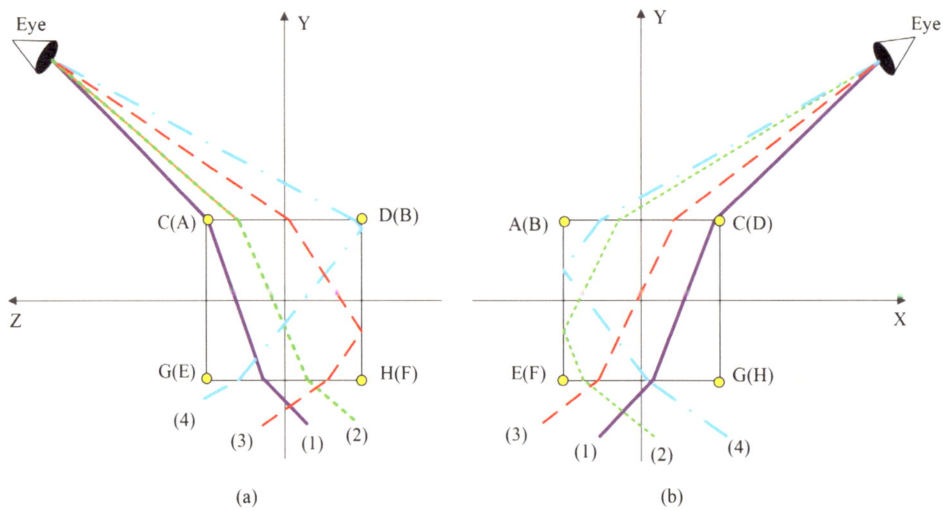

Figure 11.
Ray path in a cubed glass. (a) YZ cross section and (b) XY cross section.

indicated as (1) to (4) show the divided regions on the top plane, and in **Figure 11**, the same four numbers show four rays that pass the same regions as those in **Figure 10**. In addition, **Figure 11** shows that the numbers outside the parenthesis are near to the eye point, while the numbers inside the parenthesis are far from the eye. Each divided region in **Figure 10** has the effect of reflection and/or refraction as the following:

(1) Two refractions on the bottom and the top planes.

(2) Two refractions on the bottom and the top planes and one total reflection on the side of ABFE.

(3) Two refractions on the bottom and the top planes and one total reflection on the side of BDHF.

(4) Two refractions on the bottom and the top planes and two reflections on two sides of ABFE and BDHF.

For generation of the image drawn on the top plane of the cubed glass, we need to decide the boundary between regions. In **Figure 10**, the image is flipped on the boundary line, and the flip is caused by total reflection inside the cubed glass. For example, the region (2) has one total reflection on the side of ABFE in addition to two refractions on the bottom and the top planes. Then, the boundary line on the top plane can be decided by the ray that passes the bottom edge line (EF) of the cubed glass. In addition, the boundary line between the regions (1) and (2) or the regions (3) and (4) is parallel to Z axis, and the boundary line between the regions (1) and (3) or the regions (2) and (4) is parallel to X axis. Therefore, the searching algorithm is as follows for the boundary line that divides the regions (1) and (3) or the regions (2) and (4). **Figure 12** shows the process of the algorithm:

<Boundary line search algorithm>

1) Set A as A′ and C as C′.

2) Set the initial point P as the middle point of A′C′.

3) Calculate the refractive light with the incident and the refractive angles (θ and ϕ).

4) Calculate the intersection point of the refractive light and the line of AE, and set the point as Q.

5) If Q nearly equals to E, the line that passes P and is parallel to X axis is the boundary. Stop here.

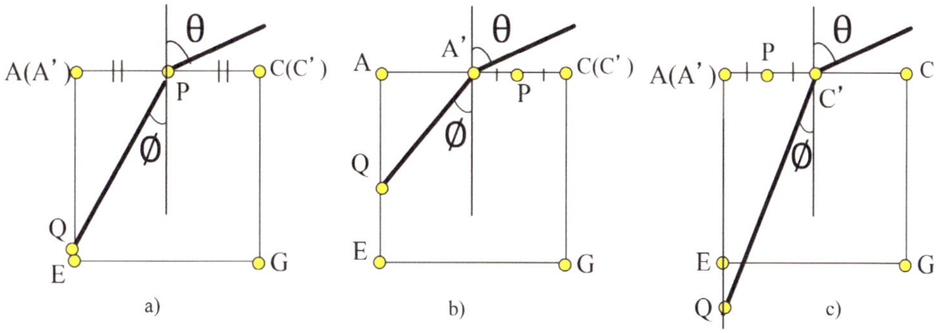

Figure 12.
Boundary line search algorithm. (a) Process of 1-5 (b) In case of AQ<AE and (c) In case of AQ>AE.

6) If the length of AQ is shorter than that of AE, set the middle point of C′P as the next point of P, and set the original P as A′. Otherwise, set the middle point of A′P as the next point of P and set the original P as C′.

4.2 Simulation with a cubed glass

Figure 13 shows the simulation result with the proposed method for the case of **Figure 10** and the comparison with the real photo. The top plane is divided into four regions, and the images on some regions are flipped due to total reflection on the side planes.

Figure 14 shows another simulation result and the real photo for an eraser that has texture on the surfaces. In this case, the front plane is divided into four regions, and some images on the regions are flipped due to total reflection. We can see that the two images are very similar.

Figure 15 shows the process to generate **Figure 14(a)**. **Figure 15(c)** is the image without reflection and refraction because the part is directly seen from the eye position and the ray does not pass the cubed glass. All images except for (c) have two refractions on the back and the front planes. The image (b) has only two refractions on the back and the front planes of the cubed glass. It does not have any total reflection. On the other hand, the image (a) has one total reflection on the side

(a) (b)

Figure 13.
Simulation result and the real photo for a string of "GRAPHICS." (a) Simulation result and (b) Real photograph.

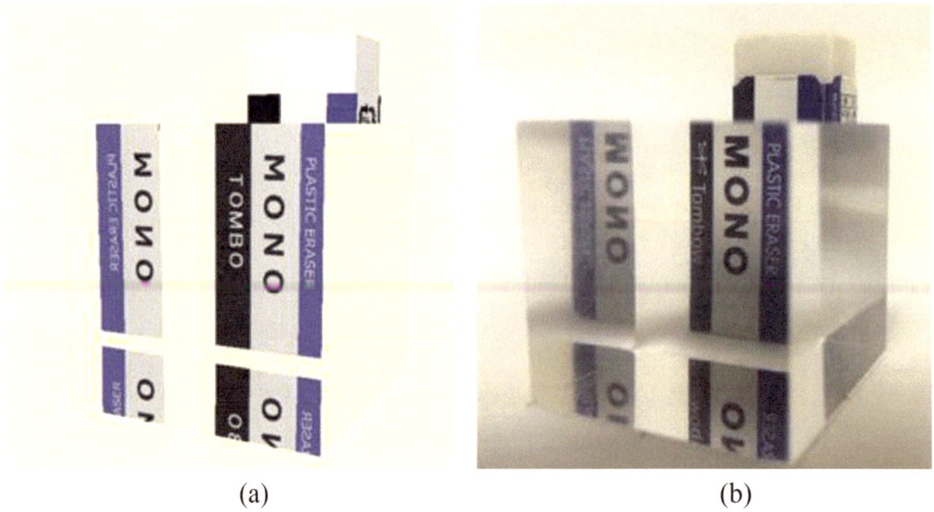

Figure 14.
Simulation result and the real photo for an eraser with texture. (a) Simulation result and (b) Real photograph.

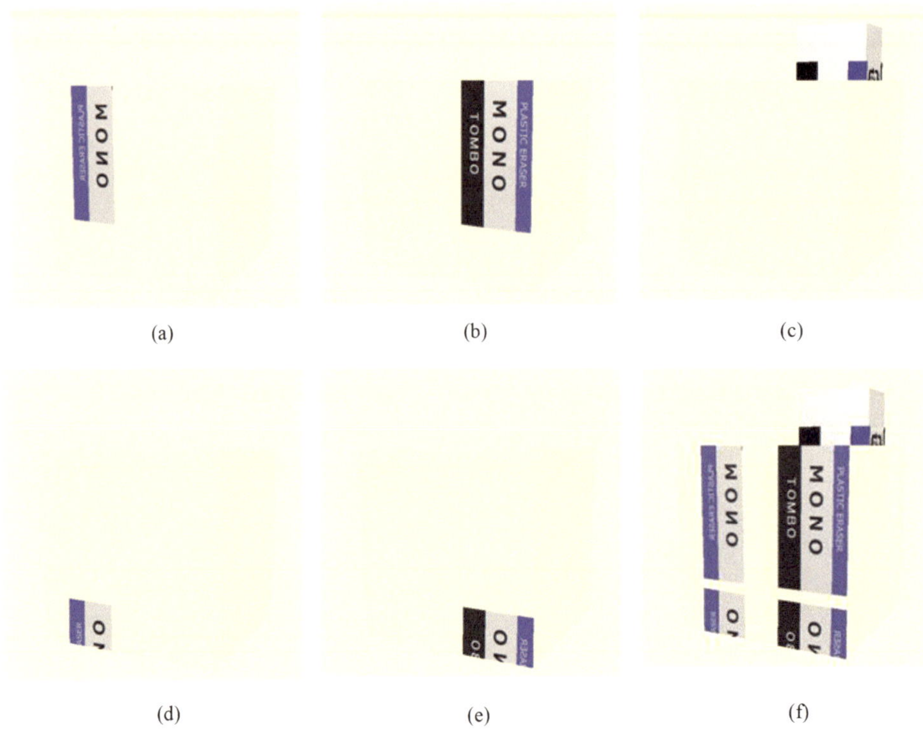

Figure 15.
Divided images and the combined image generated on one plane. (a) Reflection on side (b) No reflection (c) Image outside the class (d) Total reflections on side and bottom (e) Total reflection on bottom and (d) Combined image.

plane so that the string on the eraser is generated by flipping the image (b) horizontally. The image (e) also has only one total reflection on the bottom plane so that the image is generated by flipping the image (b) vertically. In addition, the image (d) has two total reflections on the side and the bottom so that the image is generated by flipping the image (b) horizontally and vertically. The image (f) is the

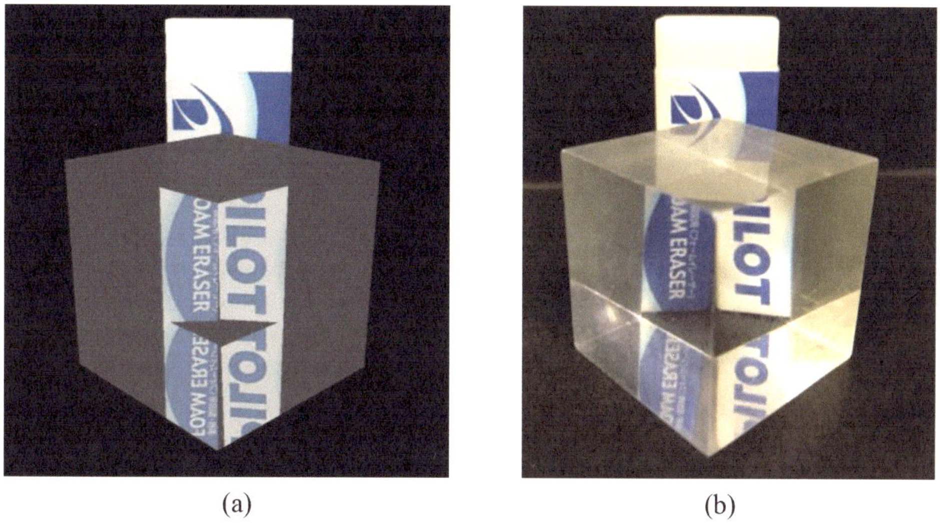

Figure 16.
Simulation result and the real photo for an image generated on three planes. (a) Simulation result and (b) Real photograph.

combined image. Then, we can understand which part is generated by reflection and/or refraction by using the proposed method.

In **Figures 13** and **14**, the simulation result has an image only on one plane: top or front. However, the method can be applied to multiple planes. **Figure 16** shows the application, where the images are generated on three planes.

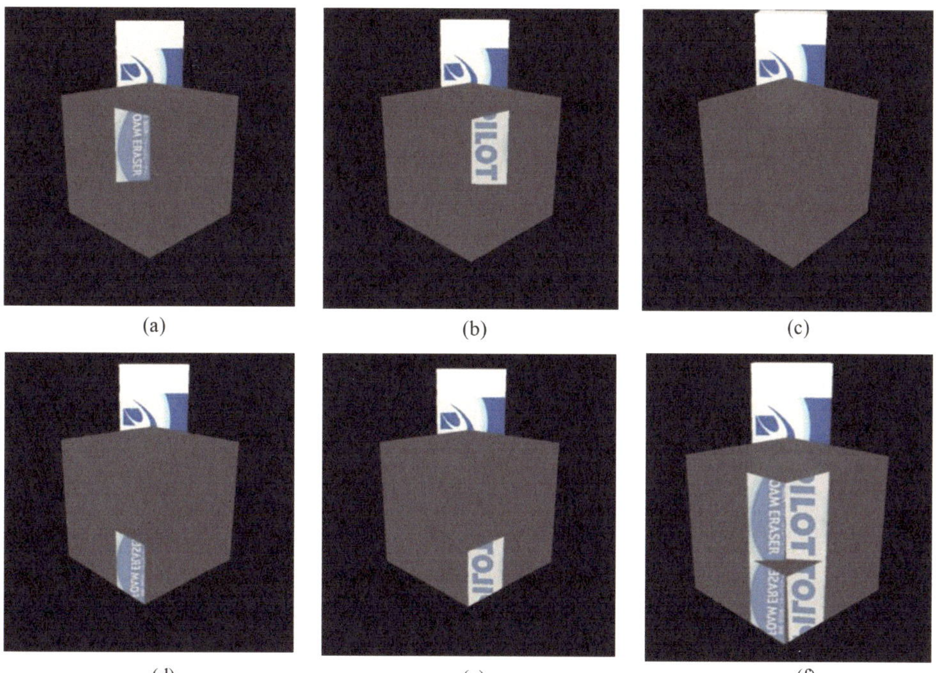

Figure 17.
Divided images and the combined image generated on three planes. (a) No reflection on left front (b) No refraction on right front (c) Direct reflection on top (d) Total reflection on left bottom (e) Total reflection on right bottom and (f) Combined image.

In addition, **Figure 17** shows the process to generate **Figure 16(a)**. In the figure, all parts have an image seen directly from the eye position, so that it has no reflection and refraction. The image (c) has no total reflection and refraction. It has only the direct reflection of the eraser on the top plane; however, it is difficult to identify it because the image is not so clear, which is the same as that of the real photo (**Figure 16(b)**). Both (a) and (b) have only two refractions; however, the refractive planes are different. The refractive planes are parallel since there is no total reflection. The one is the plane that has the image, and the other is the plane that is parallel to it. On the other hand, both (e) and (f) have one total reflection on the bottom plane so that the string on the eraser is vertically flipped. The images (d) and (e) are generated by flipping the images (a) and (b) vertically, respectively. Finally, (f) is the combined image. The process of the image generation helps us to understand which part is generated by reflection and/or refraction.

5. Cylindrical glass

5.1 Movement of virtual vertex

This section describes how to generate the image for a cylindrical glass. In the inside of a cylindrical glass, there are four refractions at the most, and the position of a virtual vertex moves dynamically. **Figure 18** shows the movement of a virtual vertex by each refraction through a cylindrical glass. In the figure, the thickness of the cylindrical glass is W, and Q is the original vertex. Vertex Q is directly seen from point D; however, the ray is refracted at point D so that the vertex cannot be directly seen from point C. If the vertex moves from Q to Q_D, it is directly seen from point C. The same movement should be done for the rest. If vertex Q_D moves to Q_C, it can be directly seen from point B, and if vertex Q_C moves to Q_B, then it can also be directly seen from point A. Finally, if vertex Q_B moves to Q_A, then it can be directly seen from the eye position.

Then, each virtual vertex can be calculated as follows. The virtual Vertex Q_D is calculated as the intersection between the line that passes C and D and another line that passes point Q and is parallel to the line OD. The remains are calculated with

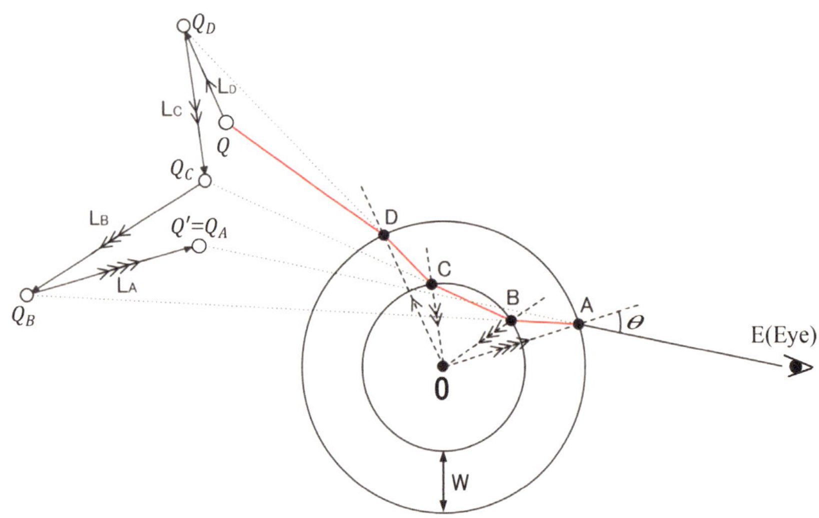

Figure 18.
Movement of a virtual vertex.

(a) (b)

Figure 19.
Simulation result and the real photo for a cylindrical glass. (a) Simulation result and (b) Real photograph.

the same method. Vertex Q_c is calculated as the intersection between the line that passes B and C and another line that passes point Q_D and is parallel to the line OC. The vertex Q_B is calculated as the intersection between the line that passes A and B and another line that passes point Q_c and is parallel to the line OB. Finally, virtual vertex $Q' = Q_A$ is solved as the intersection between the line that passes A and E and another line that passes point Q_B and is parallel to the line OA.

If the final virtual vertex Q' is obtained, we can generate the refractive image just by rendering the objects constructed with virtual vertices without considering any refraction.

5.2 Simulation with a cylindrical glass

Figure 19 shows the simulation image generated with the proposed method and the real photo. The eraser is distorted inside the cylindrical glass due to four refractions. The simulation result is very similar to the real photo, and the image can be generated in real time. That is, the simulation image changes in real time according to the movement of the real eraser.

6. Conclusion and future work

In this chapter, a new method to generate reflective and refractive images has been proposed. The method generates virtual objects that have virtual vertices translated from the original ones by considering reflection and refraction. By rendering the virtual objects, we can generate the reflective and/or refractive images without considering reflection and refraction. For the parallel glass, the calculation equations for the virtual vertex have been derived. In addition, total reflection and attenuation of light energy have been considered, and the attenuation is used as an alpha value to blend some images in alpha blending. On the other hand, the position of a virtual vertex moves dynamically for a cylindrical glass, and the position can be calculated as the intersection of two lines. Finally, the proposed method has been applied to two types of glass: cubed glass and cylindrical glass. On the both cases, the simulation results have been very similar to the real photos, and the image can be generated in real time.

The proposed method helps us to understand which part of the image is generated by refraction, reflection, or total reflection. In addition, we can understand on which plane the reflection happens or which pair of planes causes the refraction. However, by comparing the simulation results with the real photos, we see that the image quality is different, especially the transparency. Then, in order to improve the image quality, we have to try another technique such as blending the simulation result with environment map.

Author details

Nobuhiko Mukai
Tokyo City University, Tokyo, Japan

*Address all correspondence to: mukai@cs.tcu.ac.jp

References

[1] Whitted T. An improved illumination model for shaded display. In: Proceedings of the ACM SIGGRAPH; 1979. p. 14

[2] Whitted T. An improved illumination model for shaded display. Communications of the ACM. 1980; **23**(6):343-349

[3] Heckbert P, Hanrahan P. Beam tracing polygonal objects. In: Proceedings of the ACM SIGGRAPH; 1984. pp. 119-127

[4] Amanatides J. Ray tracing with cones. In: Proceedings of the ACM SIGGRAPH; 1984. pp. 129-135

[5] Blinn JF, Newell ME. Texture and reflection in computer generated images. Communications of the ACM. 1976;**19**(10):542-547

[6] Pauline T, Brian B. Modeling and rendering waves: Wave-tracing using beta-splines and reflective and refractive texture mapping. ACM Transactions on Graphics. 1987;**6**(3): 191-214

[7] Hakura Z, Snyder J, Lengyel J. Parameterized environment maps. In: Proceedings of the ACM Symposium on I3D; 2001. pp. 203-208

[8] G'enevaux O, Larue F, Dischler J. Interactive refraction on complex static geometry using spherical harmonics. In: Proceedings of the ACM Symposium on I3D; 2006. pp. 145-152

[9] Ofek E, Rappoport A. Interactive reflections on curved objects. In: Proceedings of the ACM SIGGRAPH; 1998. pp. 333-342

[10] Iwasaki K, Dobashi Y, Nishita T. A fast rendering method for refractive and reflective caustics due to water surfaces. In: Proceedings of Computer Graphics Forum. 2003;**22**(3):601-609

[11] Wang W, Wang L, Lin S, Wang J, Guo B. Real-time environment map interpolation. In: Proceedings of the 3rd International Conference on Image and Graphics; 2004. pp. 382-389

[12] Wyman C. Interactive image-space refraction of nearby geometry. In: Proceedings of the 3rd International Conference on Computer Graphics and Interactive Technique in Australasia and South Asia; 2005. pp. 205-211

[13] Hu W, Qin K. Interactive approximate rendering of reflections, refractions, and caustics. IEEE Transactions on Visualization and Computer Graphics. 2007;**13**(1):46-57

[14] Oliveira M, Brauwers M. Real-time refraction through deformable objects. In: Proceedings of the 2007 Symposium on Interactive 3D Graphics; 2007. pp. 89-96

[15] Rodgman D, Chen M. Refraction in volume graphics. Graphical Models. 2006;**68**:432-450

[16] Rousiers C, Bousseau A, Subr K, Holzchuch N, Ramamoorthi R. Real-time rendering of rough refraction. IEEE Transactions on Visualization and Computer Graphics. 2012;**18**(10): 1591-1602

[17] Chen Z, Wong KK. Depth from refraction using a transparent medium with unknown pose and refractive index. International Journal of Computer Vision. 2013;**102**(1–3):3-17

[18] Mukai N, Makino Y, Chang Y. Ray tracing based fast refraction method for an object seen through a cylindrical glass. In: Proceedings of MODSIM; 2013. pp. 747-753

[19] Mukai N, Kumagai K, Chang Y. Analytical method for generating images reflected on a cubed glass. In: Proceedings of NICOGRAPH International; 2016. pp. 178-181

Chapter 4

Topological Visualisation Techniques for Volume Multifield Data

Dean P. Thomas, Rita Borgo, Robert S. Laramee and Simon J. Hands

Abstract

This survey paper provides an overview of topological visualisation techniques for scalar data sets. Topological algorithms are used to reduce scalar fields to a skeleton by mapping critical changes in the topology to the vertices of graph structures. These can be visualised using graph drawing techniques or used as a method of seeding meshes of distinct objects existing in the data. Many techniques are discussed in detail, beginning with a review of algorithms working on scalar fields defined with a single variable, and then generalised to multivariate and temporal data. The survey is completed with a discussion of methods of presenting data in higher dimensions.

Keywords: indirect volume rendering, topology driven visualisation, multivariate visualisation, contour tree, Reeb graph, Reeb space, joint contour net, Reeb skeleton, scalar data

1. Introduction

The Marching Cubes (MC) algorithm [1] is a long established method used in indirect visualisation for creating mathematical models of data existing in a scalar field. Early research centred upon improvements for the presentation of data from medical sources such as CT and MRI scans. Whilst well suited for approximating isosurfaces on smooth functions, MC derived algorithms typically struggle to accurately capture features such as sharp edges and corners. These features can often to lead to poorly shaped triangles. Various approaches have been suggested for correcting these limitations including *Extended Marching Cubes* [2], *Dual Marching Cubes* [3], and *Cube Merging* [4]. The algorithm continues to be refined and improved for various purposes, and remains an active field of study [5].

Besides improvements to model quality, a recurring theme in research linked to the algorithm is identifying and solving topological ambiguities in the models it creates. Typical ambiguities result in the absence of triangles between two surfaces existing in opposing corners of a MC cell. This can lead to creation of a model which contains two separate objects, when in reality the model should be a single joined object. Many approaches have been suggested for overcoming these ambiguities including the use of Marching Tetrahedra [6]. The use of topological algorithms removes the possibility for ambiguities, whilst providing a method for seeding disjoint contours using similar lookup tables to those of Marching Cubes. Algorithms for surface generation, such as Marching Cubes, can also be generalised for use in multivariate data sets.

The remainder of this chapter is structured as follows. Section 2 describes topological visualisation techniques for scalar fields that solve the ambiguity problems of MC. In Section 3 we discuss extending topological techniques to cover multivariate data sets. Section 4 considers displaying the output of topological algorithms from higher dimensional data sets. The chapter is concluded in Section 5.

2. Topology driven visualisation

Algorithms for computing isosurfaces, otherwise known as level sets, are prone to topological inaccuracies [7–9]. During the construction of an isosurface no topological information is used; hence, an isosurface is unable to distinguish individual connected regions. Morse theory provides a method for computing the topology of scalar data, as we sweep through the isovalue range, by considering the gradient and second derivatives of the level set at each vertex in the scalar field. Through the use of tetrahedral mesh cells (for 3D scalar fields) we can approximate the isosurface as a piecewise linear function between sampling points. However, at the boundary between cells this approach invalidates a key condition of Morse theory which requires a function to have derivatives defined at all sampling points. Work by Edelsbrunner et al. [10] and Bremer et al. [11] provides a mechanism for handling these limitations, allowing us to consider the data as a Morse function.

Topology driven visualisation is used to capture characteristics of a data set using basic topological invariants such as the number of holes or points in a connected region. This information provides a means for obtaining a skeleton of the data which can then be used to construct visualisations in various forms. Use of topological visualisation techniques can see a reduction in the size of a large data set, as only key features need to be retained. By using topological structures to represent a data set intuitive methods can be used for speeding up computations; for example, by allowing many parts of a data set to be rendered in parallel. A further increase in efficiency is provided by the ability to bypass redundant computations—such as the processing of empty cells in MC. Increases in rendering performance come with the overhead of the need to do a one-time pre-processing of the data.

Many topology based algorithms rely on abstract graph based structures for storage of data. In many situations the graph structures can be viewed directly to form an overview of the data in an easily perceived format. For those with little prior knowledge of topological visualisation techniques it can be hard to form an initial understanding of the data using such formats. In order to better understand the data it is common to directly link the graph visualisation, either statically or dynamically, with a rendered view of the data. However, difficulty in understanding topological data representations can be further complicated when a data set is large in size. Hence, other approaches are sometimes used that try to take advantage of human perception, such as topological landscapes.

2.1 Terminology

In order to present the algorithms and structures used in topological visualisation the following key terminology is used.

2.1.1 Simplex

The simplex is a generalisation of the triangle or tetrahedron to n dimensions. Properties of simplexes in dimensions 0 (a point) through to 4 (a Pentatope) are given in **Table 1**. Computational topology often refers to meshes as simplicial complexes—a set of n simplexes glued together at their boundaries.

2.1.2 Betti numbers

Enable us to categorise the topology of a mesh existing in n dimensions by examining the connectivity of its structure as a number of n dimensional simplexes. Each dimension, from 0 to $n - 1$, has its own Betti number β_n associated with it to represent the quantity of cuts required through a mesh in order to separate it into two parts. We can consider these numbers as representing the number of holes in the mesh in n dimensions (**Table 2**). Most topological visualisation algorithms consider only the 0th dimensional Betti number, used to represent connectivity. However, it is possible to augment the graphs with higher order Betti numbers to provide feedback on changes in the mesh such as the morphing from a sphere to a torus (**Table 3**). In this work we are primarily only interested in the zeroth dimensional Betti number β_0.

2.1.3 Genus

This is a way of expressing the number of holes in a surface. In three dimensions, a sphere is genus 0, and torus genus 1. Surfaces with additional holes are commonly referred to as an n-torus.

2.1.4 Critical point

The sampling points in a scalar field $f(x)$, at which the function value is defined, can be categorised into two types. Critical points have a local gradient $f'(x) = 0$ and represent positions where the topology of the level set changes. These relate to local extrema or saddle points in the data; the second derivative $f''(x)$ allows us to classify

Name	Dimension n	Common name	Vertices	Edges	Faces	Cells
0-simplex	0	Point	1	—	—	—
1-simplex	1	Line-segment	2	1	—	—
2-simplex	2	Triangle	3	3	1	—
3-simplex	3	Tetrahedron	4	6	4	1
4-simplex	4	Pentatope (or 5-cell)	5	10	10	5

Table 1.
Classification of simplexes in dimensions zero to four.

Betti number	Associated simplex	Property
β_0	Point	Connected components
β_1	Line-segment	Holes
β_2	Triangles	Voids

Table 2.
Betti numbers β_0, β_1, and β_2 and associated concepts of connectivity.

Topological concept	β_0	β_1	β_2
Sphere	1	0	1
Torus	1	2	1

Table 3.
Betti numbers used to describe the sphere and torus.

if the critical point is a local minima $f''(x) > 0$ or a local maxima $f''(x) < 0$. In the case where a critical point is a local minima all neighbouring vertices will have a higher function value, whilst a local maxima means that all surrounding vertices are lower in value. Regular points have a non-zero gradient and have no overall effect on the connectivity the level set.

2.1.5 Contour

The boundary of connected regions of a level set, also known as the 0-dimensional homology group, is known as contours. Each individual contour is an element in the level set that represents a distinct topological object within the isosurface.

2.1.6 Topological persistence

The most simplistic way of defining topological persistence is as a quantitative measure of importance of each contour. In literature topological persistence is often known as geometric measures [12] due to the fact it relates to measures such as volume or surface area. It is possible to compute persistence values directly from the meshes representing each contour by performing a piecewise sum of all cells in a connected region. Alternatively, the persistence can be approximated by counting the number of regular vertices making up a connected region. Persistence measures are often used as a method of eliminating noise from the topological structure by iteratively removing the contour with smallest persistence value.

Most of the techniques and structures discussed in this section can be generalised for use in any number of dimensions—a list of general terms is provided in **Table 4**.

2.2 Merge trees

One of the fundamental data structures in computational topology are merge trees, commonly used to describe two similar concepts. Merge trees track connected level sets within the data as the isovalue is swept across the scalar range. The *join tree* captures connected sub-level sets, or regions, of the data below a specific isovalue threshold. Similarly the *split tree* captures connected super-level sets.

Name	Dimension	Common name
0-manifold	0	Point
1-manifold	1	Polyline
2-manifold	2	Polygon
3-manifold	3	Polyhedron
4-manifold	4	4-Polytope

Table 4.
Classification of manifolds in dimensions zero to four.

Merge trees present a simple method for capturing topological information as the arcs in a tree-like structure. This can then be used to compute zero-dimensional persistence measures representing the number of connected components in a region [14]. Merge trees are often used as a computation step in the construction of more complex topological data structures such as the contour tree, described in detail in Section 2.3. Alternatively, merge trees can be used directly for analysis and feature extraction in complex data sets [13].

A visual metaphor for understanding the concept of merge trees is given in **Figure 1**. To capture the merge tree, in this case the join tree of the grey function (top-left), the isovalue is gradually decreased from the global maxima. In the top-centre image this has revealed three local maxima, each denoted as a red critical point. In the top right image a fourth local maxima has been revealed (the green contour) and the red and blue structures have merged, this is marked by a node in the graph. In the bottom left image, the pink and green surfaces have merged to form the cyan region. The bottom centre image sees the small intervals represented by the cyan and yellow surfaces merged into one large purple region. If the isovalue continues to be reduced it is possible to observe no further changes in the topology until reaching the global minima represented by the blue graph node.

2.3 The contour tree

The contour tree, introduced by Boyell and Ruston [16] uses concepts from Morse theory [17, 18] to capture changes in the topology of scalar field at critical points in the data. The tree structure allows the tracking of splits and joins in the topology as the isovalue is varied by tracing a path through the graph. **Figure 2** demonstrates how individual contours in the data are captured by the contour tree using a one-to-one correspondence with edges. Each leaf in the contour tree represents an individual local extrema and critical vertices represent a change in the connectivity of the level set. Typically, the contour tree does not contain information regarding changes in topological genus; however, this information can be added to the output [19].

We can formally describe the structure of the contour tree as follows:

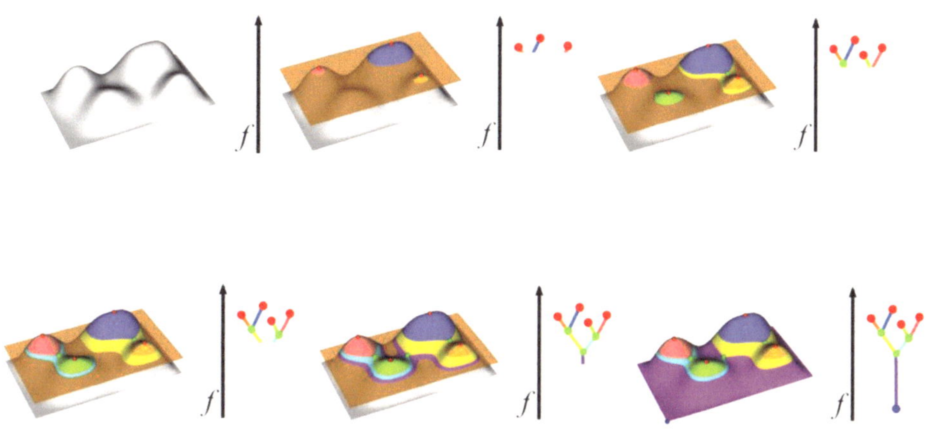

Figure 1.
A visual representation of the merge tree algorithm for the function shown in the top-left. The merge tree captures each of the local maxima as the function height is reduced (moving left-to-right, top-to-bottom). A real world analogy is to think of the isovalue as the water level in a valley that gradually drains to reveal the peaks of multiple hills. Image courtesy of Landge et al. [13].

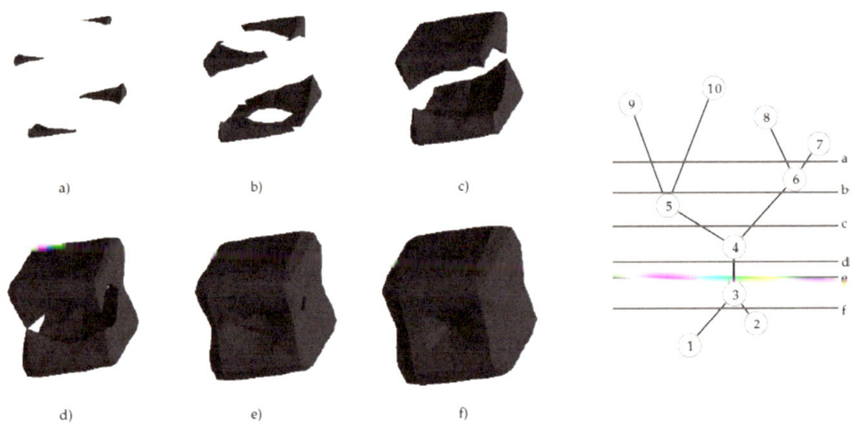

Figure 2.
Left: a surface that varies as the function value is varied. Right: a labelled contour tree representation of the surface. Image courtesy of Carr et al. [15].

- Vertices or *supernodes*
  - Leaf nodes correspond to:

    a. Local maxima where a contour is created.

    b. Local minima where a contour is destroyed.
  - Interior nodes correspond to:

    a. A saddle point where one more contours are created as a contour splits into two or more disjoint contours.

    b. A saddle point where one or more contours are destroyed as two or more disjoint contours merge into one.

- Edges or *superarcs*
  - Represent a single contour between the supernode where it is created and the supernode where it is destroyed.

In addition to optimizations of contour tree computation, research is focused on approaches for storing the contour tree hierarchy, allowing it to be traversed in an efficient manner. A number of related approaches have been proposed including Kd-trees, segment trees, and interval trees. These formats prove problematic as they can require a large amount of storage and are difficult to navigate. An alternative method is proposed in [20] using the observation that an isosurface is the level set of a continuous function in 3D space; therefore, a whole contour can be traced from a single element. Vertices where contours can be built from are given the name seeds; algorithms for computing seeds relate to work in image processing requiring similar storage facilities. An entire contour can be computed for the specified desired isovalue from the seed that is bounded by the two supernodes representing the critical points of the contour. Results showed that by using this method the number of seeds required for representation were in most cases significantly reduced. However, often the overall storage size of the contour tree was increased in comparison to other methods.

Carr et al. [15] investigated the use of contour trees in higher dimensional data sets, whilst also improving upon the algorithm proposed in [21]. This also introduced the concept of *augmented contour trees*, an extension that added non-branching vertices at non-critical points in the data to provide additional values for isosurfaces to be seeded from. This feature was built into a GUI allowing the user to identify regions of interest, using colour coding and to distinguish them as directed by the user [22]. Carr and Snoeyink [23] use the contour tree as the underlying data structure to generate object meshes using path seeds. The use of the contour tree can be extended to finding paths between two points given condition clauses, such as a minimum or maximum values, on a function defining a landscape [24].

Chiang et al. [25] introduce a modified contour tree construction algorithm that improves processing time by only sorting *critical vertices* in the merge tree construction stage. This vastly increases processing speeds in very large data sets. However, as observed by the authors, critical vertices are difficult to identify in data with dimensionality of four or more. Further increases in speed are offered by storing multiple seeds for the monotone path construction algorithm [26] used to generate surfaces. An increased storage overhead is required; however, a surface does not require complete re-extraction each time the isovalue is changed. Recently Gueunet et al. [27] presented a multithreaded approach to computing the augmented contour tree using a shared memory approach. Initial evaluations of the "contour forest" algorithm showed quicker computations achievable using the approach; however, at present the extent of the speed up is limited by load imbalance and redundant computations.

For a given technique of subdividing the input domain, the output of the contour tree algorithm is fixed. However, in the case that a different technique is used to define the neighbourhood of sampling points the location of the critical point may change trivially. For example, changing the method of defining neighbours during split/merge tree computations can slightly alter the location of critical points. The underlying structure of the tree, the number of supernodes and superarcs, remains fixed for a given input with only the geometric locations of supernodes changing.

2.4 The Reeb graph

Using the contour tree comes with the limitation that the input must be defined on a *simply connected domain* that is free of loops. Limitations in the merge tree computation phase of the contour tree algorithm prevent it from correctly handling data without a boundary. However, the Reeb graph [28], a generalisation of the contour tree, can be used to compute the topology of scalar data in such situations [29]. As with the contour tree, the Reeb graph can be applied to models of any dimension provided it is represented on a simplicial mesh [30]. The Reeb graph has also been used to assist in the design of transfer functions in volume visualisation [31], by assigning opacity based upon how many objects were obscured by nested surfaces and their proximity to the edge of a scalar field.

The first use of the Reeb graph for encoding topological features for visualisation purposes was by Shinagawa and Kunii [32] where the structure was used as a way of representing objects obtained from computerised-tomography (CT) sources [33]. An online algorithm is given by Pascucci et al. [30] that allowed the Reeb graph of a function to be computed using a streaming approach with the output continually updated as additional data points are added. Efficiency of the algorithm is optimal for two dimensional inputs and the streaming nature of the algorithm limits peak memory usage. However, the $O(n^2)$ complexity of the algorithm, where n is the number of triangles, means it performs less favourably for higher dimensional inputs.

A key feature of many Reeb graph algorithms is that a *2-skeleton* of the input volume is used to define the relationship between vertices, edges and triangles. The same restriction applies to scalar fields in n dimensions; hence, provided a triangulation of the data is available the algorithm will be able to compute a correct n dimensional Reeb graph. Reeb graph algorithms can largely be split into two groups; those that are *sweep based*, requiring the maintenance of level sets, and those that use a *split and compute* method to collapse the problem to that of a *contour tree* computation. A third alternative was given by Harvey et al. [34] that randomly collapsed triangles for arbitrary 2-skeletons to improve the running time to $O(m \log m)$.

The sensitivity of Reeb graph computations to the topological genus of the input domain was first demonstrated by McLaughlin [29] in the case of a non-simply connected domain, such as that representing a sphere or torus. Additionally, the number of loops present in the data as a result of the Morse function can further extend the complexity of the algorithm. In order to address this undesired effect the Reeb graph computation can be reduced to that of the simpler contour tree algorithm. This approach was first used by Tierny et al. [35] where they performed "loop-surgery" by making symbolic cuts during the *merge tree* step of the algorithm. The symbolic cuts could then be stitched back together to retrieve a topologically correct Reeb graph of the data. An alternative approach, capable of generalising to higher dimensional inputs, was later proposed by Doraiswamy and Natarajan [36] that explicitly maintained level sets, eliminating the need for a loop-surgery pre-processing step.

More recently Doraiswamy and Natarajan [37] offered an improved algorithm for constructing the Reeb graph of n-dimensional scalar fields, reverting to the split and compute contour tree technique, as originally proposed in [35]. A further optimised algorithm [38], using a variation of the split and compute technique, used the join tree of the data to identify potential loops. An important modification upon the technique developed by Tierny et al. [35] was the segmentation of domain into multiple loop free contour trees, instead of a single contour tree, thus enabling multiple regions of the input to be computed in parallel.

Output from Reeb graph algorithms remains fixed provided the simplicial subdivision defined upon the input domain does not change. As is the case with the contour tree, variations can slightly alter the location of the critical vertices without changing the overall structure of the graph.

2.5 Seeded contours

Contours, as opposed to isosurfaces, can be grown using values extracted from the scalar field to produce topologically correct meshes. De Berg and van Kreveld [24] made the observation that a whole contour could be traced starting from a single *seed* element. Wyvill et al. [39] generate contour surfaces as a two-stage process; first, the core region is flood filled by evaluating neighbouring cells for inclusion in the level set. In the second stage boundaries are calculated using look-up tables similar in form to those of the MC algorithm [1].

Contour trees are a reliable source of seed cells for propagation algorithms similar to those of Wyvill et al. [39]; hence, the contour tree can be used to generate surfaces for each superarc at a given isovalue. Carr and Snoeyink [23] use the contour tree as the underlying data structure to store and generate object meshes. Rather than using *minimal seed sets* as used by van Kreveld et al. [20] to generate contours, an alternative method was deployed using *path seeds*. Carr et al. [15] also investigated the use of contour trees in higher dimensional datasets, whilst also improving upon the algorithm proposed by Tarasov and Vyalyi [21]. This enables users to identify individual contours of interest and distinguish them accordingly [22].

The *flexible isosurface* [40] is a technique for combining many of the features discussed in this section with the concepts of *topological persistence* (see Section 2.6) into a single interface. Simplification methods, as discussed in [12], can also be applied to the data so as to display isosurfaces in a meaningful way. This approach allows each contour to be hidden or displayed according to the user preferences at runtime. In order to further aid data exploration contours can also remain fixed in view as the global isovalue is varied. Colour can be applied to each surface (or a sub-tree of the main contour tree) to allow assignment of meaning to contours by the user by providing a simple grouping mechanism.

2.6 Topological persistence and simplification

Different scientific fields of study often define the interesting features and attributes in a domain specific form. However, some features are invariant and can be useful in any field of science. The contour spectrum [41] was introduced as a method of relaying quantitative information about individual contours in scalar data including surface area and volume. Carr et al. [42] directly compare isosurface statistics against raw histograms of scalar data for a number of data sets. Measurements evaluated included the cell intersection count, triangle count and isosurface area. It was found that using these measures a truer distribution of the scalar field could be computed. An improvement was given by Meyer et al. [43] using concepts from geometric measure theory that minimised the effect of noise on the observed distributions. The key to this improvement was introducing a normalisation of the individual contour statistics to the domain average.

Scalar field data often contains noise; when partitioned using a topology sensitive algorithm this manifests in the generation of a large quantity of small objects present at a limited range of isovalues. Methods for reducing noise were first proposed by Edelsbrunner et al. [14] using an iterative process that performed topological simplification by assessing the Betti-numbers of topological objects. The goal of the algorithm is to simplify shape whilst preserving the underlying topological features of data existing on a triangular mesh.

Carr et al. [12] proposed the use of concepts originally discussed as part of the contour spectrum [41], such as enclosed volume and surface area, as an aid for noise removal. Objects are queued in ascending order, according to the user selected measure, and iteratively removed until a terminating level of simplification is achieved. The effects of three different simplification features are compared using X-ray data from a human skull, where it was found that use of the isovalue range persistence measure (**Figure 3**) could result in the removal of important features such as the eyes. Carr et al. remark that simplification techniques are sensitive to the source and should be chosen using domain specific knowledge. The technique is suited to n dimensional data; however, time variate data requires additional considerations in the simplification process due to connectivity between time steps.

2.7 Topology in direct volume rendering

The techniques discussed in Section 2.5 model topological objects as meshes, meaning they are well suited to indirect volume visualisation. However, topology based approaches can also be applied to data displayed using direct volume rendering approaches.

A segmentation algorithm, such as the contour tree or *volume skeleton tree*, is first used to look for boundaries between objects in the scalar field topology. Following this, traditional direct volume rendering techniques can be applied to the data based upon attributes of the identified objects. Takeshima et al. [44] use attributes such as the number of equal valued contours and occlusion to assign levels of opacity to objects. The net effect was that the outermost objects were assigned lower opacities so as to not obscure features centred in the volume. A more flexible approach was

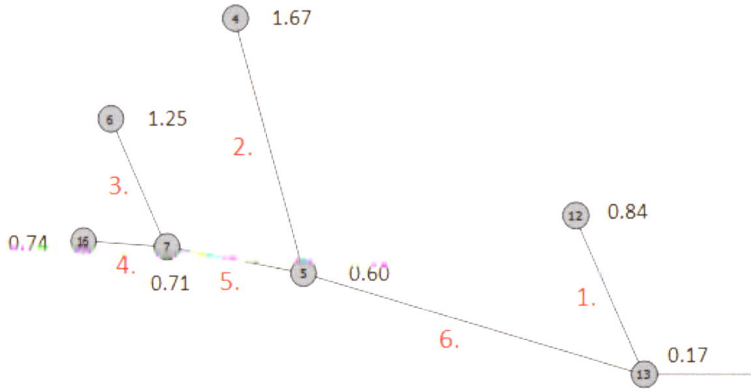

Figure 3.
An example of a topological persistence measure defined on the superarcs of a contour tree or Reeb graph. The measure of persistence defined here uses the isovalue range—this is given as the difference of isovalues of the two critical vertices defining the superarc (see **Table 5***).*

used by Weber et al. [45] applying distinct transfer functions to each object, or topological zone, as directed by the user. This customization, implemented via the user interface, enables grouping of similar features and related components using colour and transparency.

2.8 Temporal univariate scalar data

Recent interest in topological visualisation research has focused upon the comparison of scalar data through topological methods to assign a degree of similarity to data. This has potential uses in different scientific domains including physics, chemistry, and climate science, which often feature a temporal component. The merge tree, with its simple data-structure, presents an attractive method for computing topological differences between data sets. Beketayev et al. [46] define a distance measure between merge trees with potential applications in a range of scientific disciplines. The algorithm uses a *branch decomposition* approach to deconstruct the merge tree into multiple sub-graphs, each a descending path from a saddle to a leaf vertex. Each branch decomposition can then be scored via an adapted form of the edit distance [47] between two graphs. A recursive algorithm then tests if two merge trees are within an epsilon value to determine if they are classified as similar.

This approach was further extended by Saikia et al. [48] to produce the *extended branch decomposition graph*, a union of all individual sub-trees. This data structure allows quicker comparison between merge trees by computing multiple similarity thresholds in parallel. In addition the extended branch decomposition graph improves upon memory usage by reducing the redundancy found in multiple disjoint branch decompositions. Branch decomposition methods have also been applied to the more complex contour tree to compute similarity and symmetry in scalar topology [49].

The method used by Beketayev et al. [46] had a runtime of $O(n^5)$, where a merge tree contains n nodes, this was lowered to $O((n \log n)^2)$ in related work [48]. Potential downfalls to the optimised algorithm are that instabilities can arise from permuted forms of branch decompositions, this is handled in [46] by considering all possible permutations at the cost of scalability. The optimised algorithm uses the *extended branch decomposition graph*, a union of all possible branch decomposition graphs, to store all branch decompositions in a single tree structure. Two potential uses for the

Superarc		Top supernode		Bottom supernode	
Id	**Persistence**	**Id**	**Isovalue**	**Id**	**Isovalue**
1	0.67	12	0.84	13	0.17
2	1.07	4	1.67	5	0.60
3	0.54	6	1.25	7	0.71
4	0.03	16	0.74	7	0.71
5	0.11	7	0.71	5	0.60
6	0.43	5	0.60	13	0.17

Table 5.
Persistence measures associated with **Figure 3**.

distance measure are suggested; identification of similar structures within a single data set or, for time variate data, repetition between time steps.

Fluid dynamics is an area of science that can benefit from visualisation of 3D volumes with a time component. The complexity of mixing two fluids is one specific problem that can be better understood using topological methods as the system evolves over time [50]. Topological analysis makes it possible to take a slice of the volume at a given time-step and count the number of bubbles present. Alternatively, topological analysis enables tracing of properties, such the volume and centre of gravity of individual bubbles, throughout the simulation.

3. Multivariate topological visualisation

Multivariate topological visualisation is a more recent research interest in the visualisation community in comparison to topological visualisations of a single field. Due to the relative infancy of the field, Carr et al. [51] highlight the need for sufficiently complex data sets to extensively test the emerging algorithms in the area.

Many of the topological structures and algorithms applicable to a single variable can be generalised to more than one variable being defined at each sampling point. We begin this section by defining the concept of *Jacobi nodes*, we then continue to examine structures used to capture and the display the topology of multiple variables.

3.1 Jacobi node

These are critical points in the scalar fields where the gradients of multiple inputs become parallel or equal to zero. A pre-requisite for the algorithms are that the fields are defined on a common sampling mesh meaning that the critical points are guaranteed to have the same geometric locations.

3.2 The Reeb space

The *Reeb space* is a generalisation of the Reeb graph to allow for multivariate or temporal data. The first discussion of using the Reeb space to compute topological structure of multiple functions is presented by Edelsbrunner et al. [52], where it is suggested that the Reeb space can be modelled mathematically in the form $f: \mathbb{M} \mapsto \mathbb{R}^k$, where $\mathbb{M}$ represents the domain and f the output of k scalar functions. For the simple case, where $k = 1$, this is directly comparable to the Reeb graph. The Reeb space extends this formulation to situations where $k \geq 2$.

3.3 The joint contour net

Carr et al. [53] presented the first discrete representation of the Reeb space using the *Joint Contour Net* (JCN). For functions of n variables defined in an $\mathbb{R}^m$ dimensional space the algorithm approximates the Reeb space as a number of multivariate contours named joint contour slabs. These represent connected regions of the domain with respect to the isovalue of multiple functions. In situations where $n \geq m$ the JCN can still be computed; however, the output is not an approximation of the Reeb space but instead a subdivision of the input geometry over n variables. The JCN captures the Reeb space as an undirected graph structure, where vertices represent slabs of n isovalue tuples, and edges are used to show adjacency between regions. An example JCN of two scalar functions is presented in **Figures 4** and 5.

In comparison to contour tree algorithms, the JCN is better suited to parallelisation as each joint contour slab is constructed from smaller independent regions called fragments [54]. Existing development of the algorithm has focused largely on implementation as a parallel algorithm. A distributed memory model is used by Duke and Hosseini [55] to construct multiple sub-JCNs in parallel, these are merged into a single output as a final post-processing step. Current results suggest that the merge step is the limiting factor to parallel algorithm speed up; therefore, other parallelisation strategies are under investigation.

In nuclear physics the JCN has previously been used to visualise and analyse scission datasets where it was used to identify the splitting of an atomic nucleus into multiple parts [56]. It was found that the JCN was well suited to capturing this divergent behaviour using proton and neutron density fields as inputs. This experiment was initially performed at a single temperature [57], but later repeated

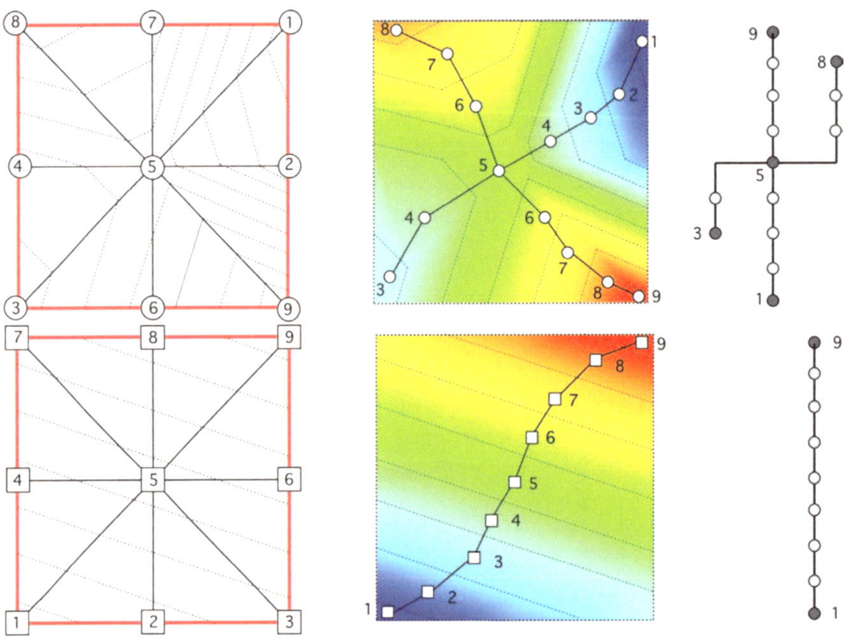

Figure 4.
Two simple scalar functions are defined on a simplicial grid (left), where the dotted lines represent quantisation intervals. The quantised contour tree for each function (right) is shown mapped to the scalar field in the Centre. Image courtesy of Duke et al. [56].

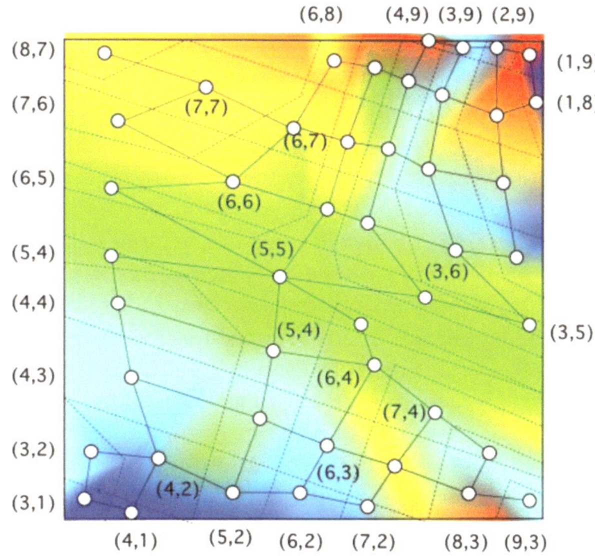

Figure 5.
A JCN capturing the bivariate topology of the two simple functions shown in **Figure 4**. *The bivariate field is constructed by overlaying the quantisation intervals of the two input fields (dotted lines). A vertex is placed at the barycentre of each region, or joint contour slab, and edges mark adjacency. Image courtesy of Duke et al. [56].*

at multiple temperatures [58] due to its ability to capture the splitting of the compound nucleus as a forking in the multi-field topology. Whilst performing the analysis a number of other events were captured and linked to the scission theory.

More recently the JCN was used to visually analyse data from hurricane Isabel [59]. Vertices were used to represent the joint contour slabs by mapping to their barycentric spatial coordinates. An interactive environment was developed that allowed users to relate interactions in the temperature, pressure and precipitation fields to physical phenomena such as rain bands and the eye of the hurricane. The ability to relate properties of the JCN to known physical features helped to increase understanding of how the JCN is able to capture multi-field interactions.

3.4 Related topological structures

In multivariate topology a *Jacobi set* represents the set of critical points generated when one Morse function is restricted to the level set of another. Alternatively, the Jacobi set can be considered as the set of points where there is an alignment of the gradient of two or more Morse functions or the gradient of one function vanishes. The similarity between two or more functions can be evaluated using the resulting Jacobi set using a method defined by Edelsbrunner et al. [60]. Applications of the Jacobi set include use as a feedback loop on simulation parameters or to perform comparison of algorithms. An algorithm was presented by Edelsbrunner and Harer [61] for computing Jacobi sets of multiple Morse functions defined on a triangular mesh of isovalue n-tuples in Euclidean space. This allows multiple independent functions such as pressure, temperature, or wind speed to be used as inputs. Alternatively for temporal data multiple time-steps can be used as input to allow the evaluation of a function with respect to time.

Carr et al. extend the JCN [53] to extract further topological structure from the Reeb space by first evaluating an intermediate structure, the *Multi-Dimensional Reeb graph* (MDRG) [62]. This is a hierarchical structure that recursively stores the joint contours of each function (f_1,f_2, ...,f_n) restricted to the contours of those preceding it. At the top level the MDRG represents the contours of the function f_1 as a Reeb Graph; the second tier relates to the Reeb graph of function f_2 when restricted to the contours of f_1, continuing down to function f_n restricted to the contours of $f_1, ..., f_{n-1}$. Besides being used in the extraction of the Jacobi structure and the related *Reeb skeleton* [63], the MDRG represents a convenient structure for extracting the Reeb graphs of each individual function making up the Reeb space.

An additional abstraction, the *Jacobi structure*, related to the mathematical topology concept of *singular fibre-components* is introduced by Chattopadhyay et al. [62] as part of the MDRG extraction algorithm. This represents an improvement over the Jacobi set by providing a method of relating the Jacobi set directly to the Reeb space. The Jacobi structure is able to capture the exact location of topological change and is defined as the projection of the Jacobi set from the domain to the Reeb space. In practice this extends the Jacobi set to also include the “regular sheets” connecting one another in the Reeb space. This means the Jacobi structure is able to capture elements of the topological structure that the Jacobi set is unable to represent. The Jacobi structure is extracted as the set of critical nodes in the Multi-Dimensional Reeb Graph (MDRG), itself a structure for storing Reeb space criticalities. Forking in multi-field topology in nuclear scission data is an example behaviour that can be captured by the Jacobi structure [62].

The *Layered Reeb graph* is an alternative approach deployed by Strodthoff and Jüttler [64] for presenting the Reeb space of multiple scalar functions. This approach to representing the Reeb space differs from the MDRG [62] by working directly with the Jacobi sets, rather than the more recently proposed Jacobi structure.

3.5 Topological persistence and simplification

Persistence in multivariate data sets is more complex to define in comparison to the univariate case. Simplification and persistence metrics can be defined on a number of secondary structures computable from the multi-field topology. The concept of isosurface statistics [42, 43] is extended to multivariate inputs through the use of *Continuous Scatterplots* [65]. These can be defined to show relations between m dimensional inputs with n scalar fields; in the case where $m = 3$ and $n = 1$ the output approximates to the output of Meyer et al. [43].

Multivariate data gives rise to *multi-filtrations* due to their parametrisation by more than one variable; this leads to no definable compact invariants, such as the Betti numbers, existing in multi-fields. Therefore, existing concepts, such as the persistence bar code [66], do not directly generalise to multi-variate domains. However, this does not mean that persistence and simplification cannot be applied, instead other approaches have been suggested. The “rank invariant” is a method for representing persistence in a multi-field by generalising upon the concept of Betti numbers present in univariate topology. For the univariate case, the rank invariant and persistence bar code are the same [67]. The original algorithm used to compute the rank invariant was exponential in time complexity, this was later improved to polynomial time by reformulating the problem as an algebraic geometry problem [68].

The Jacobi set, where the gradient of multiple functions align or have a gradient of zero, can assist in defining persistence measures [60]. When the multi-field is used to represent temporal data this can be used to augment the univariate notion of persistence with a lifetime parameter. This approach was used by Bremer et al. [69]

to compute persistence in the context of the Morse-Smale complex. However, when generalised to non-temporal functions defining persistence as a feature of the Jacobi set becomes a non-trivial task [70].

3.6 The Reeb skeleton

The Reeb skeleton (**Figure 6**) is a simplified graph structure that takes into account the size of connected components, allowing measures of persistence to be assigned to its arcs. An extended Jacobi set, the *Jacobi Structure*, is used by the Reeb skeleton algorithm to aid multivariate simplification [63].

The Jacobi structure [62] is a promising starting point for simplification due to its ability to separate the Reeb space, as approximated by the JCN, into singular and *regular components*. Just as in the univariate equivalent, the Reeb graph, singular nodes in the Jacobi structure map to topological changes in the multi-field. To exploit this, the Reeb skeleton extends the concept of the Jacobi structure further, primarily to aid multi-dimensional simplification [63].

The Reeb skeleton is generated as the dual graph of the singular and regular components captured in the Jacobi structure. Visually, this means the Reeb skeleton translates the sheet-like form of the Jacobi structure into a simplified skeletal form. The simplified graph data structure allows measures of persistence to be assigned to arcs of the Reeb skeleton in a similar manner to that of the Reeb graph. Lip pruning techniques, similar to the leaf pruning method of simplification found in univariate topological structures [12] can then be applied to progressively remove noisy features in the multi-field. Example persistence measures that can be applied to the JCN include the accumulated volume of joint contour slabs in a connected region.

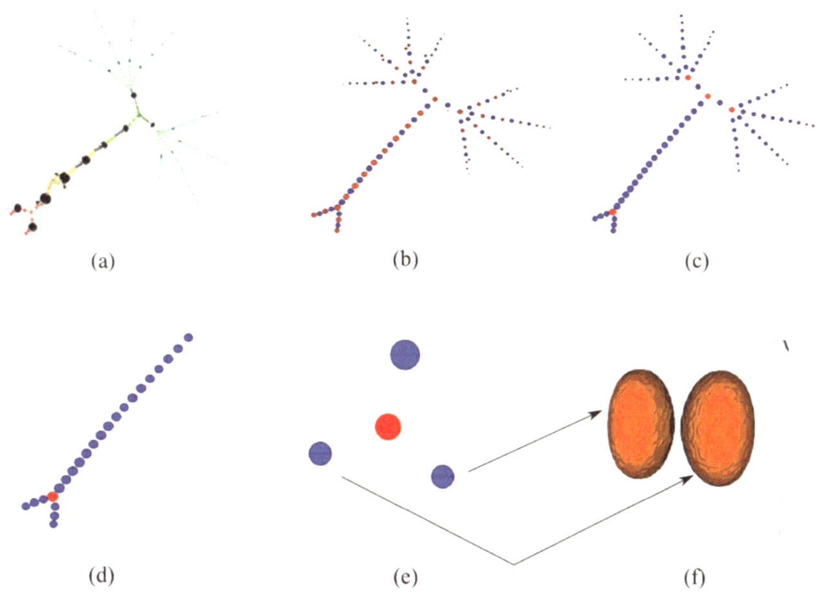

Figure 6.
An example of a Reeb skeleton, showing how it relates to the JCN (a); (b) shows the full, non-simplified Reeb skeleton; (c) modifies the Reeb skeleton to highlight only critical changes in the multivariate topology (red vertices); (d) shows how performing simplification using the Reeb skeleton removes less significant regions of the topology; (e) after simplification, the Reeb skeleton can be reduced to only key vertices; (f) the arrowed regions relate to the two surfaces. Image courtesy of Chattopadhyay et al. [63].

4. Visualisation in higher dimensions

When moving to higher dimensional spaces it is beneficial to generalise the terminology used to describe the geometry. The n-dimensional analogue of the square is the *hypercube*, often shortened to n-cube (see **Table 6**). When working in higher dimensional spaces it is common to perform a simplicial sub-division of the n-cube into n-simplexes, this helps to avoid the ambiguities often associated with MC style algorithms [71].

4.1 Projection and perception

Creating easily perceivable and topologically correct three-dimensional models for projection on to flat surfaces, the computer monitor, is a difficult task. Volumes of data become increasingly hard to visualise as their dimensionality increase; for example, by introducing a temporal fourth-dimension. One of the major limiting factors is our in ability to perceive things four-dimensionally. A metaphor for trying to understand four-dimensions in a three-dimensional world is to consider the case of two-dimensional creatures trying to understand a three-dimensional world. This is a thought exercise discussed in [72], which also discusses how a four-dimensional Euclidean representation of space-time relates to real world physics.

Existing projection methods are available that take a four-dimensional objects and display them on a two-dimensional surface, usually in wire-frame form. Quite often the projections are animated to show the object as it rotates on one or more axis; however, this can also be adapted to allow the user to rotate the object through conventional approaches such as mouse interaction. The effect of perspective and isometric projection are explored by Hollasch [73] using tesseracts—the 4D hyper-cube. In addition, the use of ray-tracing in four-dimensions can produce understandable images, as depth cueing is handled automatically by the algorithm in the creation of shadows. However, the added complexity of a fourth dimension in a looping ray tracing algorithm makes it time consuming and potentially unworkable for real time display.

4.2 Computing surfaces in higher dimensions

Whilst presenting difficulties with regard to visualisation, it can be beneficial to compute surfaces in higher dimensions. This is especially true in the case of volumetric data with a temporal element; animation can often be used to reconstruct this form of data but that presents its own perceptual issues. Computation of isosurfaces on fields existing in $\mathbb{R}^4$ space can help to improve animations by providing interpolation between discrete time-steps, resulting in smoother and easier to perceive animations. Alternatively the high-dimensional topology can be sliced along arbitrary axes to provide a snap-shot with a reduction in dimension (e.g. $\mathbb{R}^4 \mapsto \mathbb{R}^3$).

Name	Dimension n	Common name	Vertices	Edges	Faces	Cells
0-cube	0	Point	1	—	—	—
1-cube	1	Line-segment	2	1	—	—
2-cube	2	Square	4	4	1	—
3-cube	3	Cube	8	12	6	1
4-cube	4	Tesseract	16	32	24	8

Table 6.
Properties of hypercubes in dimensions zero to four.

n	Centroid division ($2^{n-1}n!$)	$n!$
2	4	2
3	24	6
4	192	24
5	1920	120
6	23,040	720

Table 7.
Number of simplexes generated using differing sub-division techniques in n dimensions.

An unavoidable consequence of upping the dimensionality of the input field is an increase in the complexity of its storage and computation. An early example of computing surfaces in > 3 dimensions is considered by Weigle and Banks [74] using a recursive technique to split n-dimensional cells into n-simplexes. The resulting surfaces exist in four dimensions and are able to be displayed using two techniques; stereographic projection (Section 4.1) or slicing to reduce dimensionality. It is noted that the centroid division technique used to break cells into simplexes used in this work is suboptimal (see **Table 7**), but can be improved using lookup tables similar to those used in marching cubes. The technique was used in [75] to compute the swept volumes of time-varying data generated from electromagnetic field simulations, allowing them to be displayed as animations.

Extending MC into the fourth dimension, and beyond, was explored by Bhaniramka et al. [76]. At the time of the report, a relatively small amount of work had been conducted in studying isosurfaces beyond the third dimension. It was found that by extending MC into 4 dimensions the look-up table, following removal of symmetrical configurations, required 222 separate configurations. As with the 3D variation of MC, one aspect to be taken into consideration is the dealing of ambiguous configurations; a mathematical proof of correctness is provided to verify that the topological structures generated are valid. An example use of this algorithm would be to present volume data with a time dimension by selecting three-dimensional slices of the hyper-volume.

4.3 Topological landscapes

An alternative approach of viewing contour information, the topological landscape, was proposed by Weber et al. [45], using the contour tree to build a 3D terrain model (**Figure 7**). The purpose of this is to harness the natural ability that

Figure 7.
Peaks within a topological landscape (left) correspond to distinct topological features in the direct volume render (right). Image courtesy of Weber et al. [45].

humans have in understanding terrain structure and use it to provide an easier to understand model of the underlying data topology. Valleys in the terrain illustrate events where a contour splits into two or more parts and peaks represent where two or more contours merge. Topological landscapes can be applied to contour trees of any number of dimensions; hence, they can provide a useful method for exploring what is happening in high dimensional data sets. The topological landscape methodology was further expanded using a number of different methods for laying out the data, primarily from established 2D visualisation techniques [77].

5. Conclusion

In this chapter we first considered problems existing in marching cubes algorithms relating to the topological correctness of the data. We demonstrated how, through the use of topology, a correct representation of a scalar field can be captured using graph structures. These could be used to seed topologically correct meshes for rendering, or to provide a means to analyse the data. After providing a description of algorithms for data sets consisting of a single variable, we showed how many of the techniques can be generalised to multivariate data. Finally, we considered the techniques for displaying data existing in higher dimensions.

Acknowledgements

This work used the resources of the DiRAC Facility jointly funded by STFC, the Large Facilities Capital Fund of BIS and Swansea University, and the DEISA Consortium (www.deisa.eu), funded through the EU FP7 project RI-222919, for support within the DEISA Extreme Computing Initiative. The work was also partly funded by EPSRC project: EP/M008959/1. The authors would also like to thank Dr. Hamish Carr for his advice and assistance throughout the duration of this work.

Author details

Dean P. Thomas[1,2]*, Rita Borgo[3], Robert S. Laramee[1] and Simon J. Hands[2]

1 Department of Computer Science, Swansea University, Swansea, United Kingdom

2 Department of Physics, Swansea University, Swansea, United Kingdom

3 Department of Informatics, Kings College London, London, United Kingdom

*Address all correspondence to: 798295@swansea.ac.uk

References

[1] Lorensen WE, Cline HE. Marching cubes: A high resolution 3D surface construction algorithm. Computer Graphics (Proceedings of SIGGRAPH 87). 1987;**21**(4):163-169

[2] Kobbelt LP, Botsch M, Schwanecke U, Seidel H-P. Feature sensitive surface extraction from volume data. In: Proceedings of the 28th Annual Conference on Computer Graphics and Interactive Techniques. 2001. pp. 57-66

[3] Nielson GM. Dual marching cubes. In: Proceedings of the Conference on Visualization'04. 2004. pp. 489-496

[4] Bhattacharya A, Wenger R. Constructing isosurfaces with sharp edges and corners using cube merging. Computer Graphics Forum. 2013;**32**(3pt1):11-20

[5] Newman TS, Yi H. A survey of the marching cubes algorithm. Computers and Graphics. 2006;**30**(5):854-879

[6] Zhou Y, Chen W, Tang Z. An elaborate ambiguity detection method for constructing isosurfaces within tetrahedral meshes. Computers and Graphics. 1995;**19**(3):355-364

[7] Dürst MJ. Re: Additional reference to marching cubes. ACM SIGGRAPH Computer Graphics. 1988;**22**(5):243

[8] Lewiner T, Lopes H, Vieira AW, Tavares G. Efficient implementation of marching cubes' cases with topological guarantees. Journal of Graphics Tools. 2003;**8**(2):1-15

[9] Etiene T et al. Topology verification for isosurface extraction. IEEE Transactions on Visualization and Computer Graphics. 2012;**18**(6):952-965

[10] Edelsbrunner H, Harer J, Zomorodian A. Hierarchical Morse complexes for piecewise linear 2-manifolds. In: Proceedings of the Seventeenth Annual Symposium on Computational Geometry. 2001. pp. 70-79

[11] Bremer P-T, Edelsbrunner H, Hamann B, Pascucci V. A multi-resolution data structure for two-dimensional Morse-Smale functions. In: Proceedings of the 14th IEEE Visualization 2003 (VIS'03). 2003. p. 19

[12] Carr H, Snoeyink J, van de Panne M. Simplifying flexible isosurfaces using local geometric measures. In: Proceedings of the Conference on Visualization'04. 2004. pp. 497-504

[13] Landge AG et al. In-situ feature extraction of large scale combustion simulations using segmented merge trees. In: High Performance Computing, Networking, Storage and Analysis, SC14: International Conference for. 2014. pp. 1020-1031

[14] Edelsbrunner H, Letscher D, Zomorodian A. Topological persistence and simplification. Discrete and Computational Geometry. 2002;**28**(4):511-533

[15] Carr H, Snoeyink J, Axen U. Computing contour trees in all dimensions. Computational Geometry. 2003;**24**:75-94

[16] Boyell RL, Ruston H. Hybrid techniques for real-time radar simulation. In: Proceedings of the November 12-14, 1963, Fall Joint Computer Conference. 1963. pp. 445-458

[17] Banchoff T et al. Critical points and curvature for embedded polyhedra. Journal of Differential Geometry. 1967;**1**(3-4):245-256

[18] Freeman H, Morse SP. On searching a contour map for a given terrain

elevation profile. Journal of the Franklin Institute. 1967;**284**(1):1-25

[19] Pascucci V, Cole-McLaughlin K. Efficient computation of the topology of level sets. In: Proceedings of the Conference on Visualization'02. 2002. pp. 187-194

[20] van Kreveld M, van Oostrum R, Bajaj C, Pascucci V, Schikore D. Contour trees and small seed sets for isosurface traversal. In: Proc. Thirteen. Annu. Symp. Comput. Geom.—SCG '97. 1997. pp. 212-220

[21] Tarasov SP, Vyalyi MN. Construction of contour trees in 3D in O (n log n) steps. In: Proceedings of the Fourteenth Annual Symposium on Computational Geometry. 1998. pp. 68-75

[22] Carr H, Van Panne M. Topological Manipulation of Isosurfaces. Canada: The University of British Columbia; 2004

[23] Carr H, Snoeyink J. Path seeds and flexible isosurfaces using topology for exploratory visualization. In: Proceedings of the Symposium on Data Visualisation 2003. 2003. pp. 49-58

[24] De Berg M, van Kreveld M. Trekking in the Alps without freezing or getting tired. Algorithmica. 1997;**18**:306-323

[25] Chiang Y-J, Lenz T, Lu X, Rote G. Simple and optimal output-sensitive construction of contour trees using monotone paths. Computational Geometry. 2005;**30**(2): 165-195

[26] Takahashi S, Ikeda T, Shinagawa Y, Kunii TL, Ueda M. Algorithms for extracting correct critical points and constructing topological graphs from discrete geographical elevation data. Computer Graphics Forum. 1995;**14**(3):181-192

[27] Gueunet C, Fortin P, Jomier J, Tierny J. Contour forests: Fast multi-threaded augmented contour trees. 2016

[28] Reeb G. Sur les points singuliers d'une forme de pfaff completement integrable ou d'une fonction numerique [on the singular points of a completely integrable pfaff form or of a numerical function]. Comptes Rendus de l'Académie des Sciences. 1946;**222**:847-849

[29] Cole-McLaughlin K, Edelsbrunner H, Harer J, Natarajan V, Pascucci V. Loops in Reeb graphs of 2-manifolds. In: Proceedings of the Nineteenth Annual Symposium on Computational Geometry. 2003. pp. 344-350

[30] Pascucci V, Scorzelli G, Bremer P-T, Mascarenhas A. Robust on-line computation of Reeb graphs: Simplicity and speed. ACM Transactions on Graphics (TOG). 2007;**26**(3):58

[31] Fujishiro I, Takeshima Y, Azuma T, Takahashi S. Volume data mining using 3D field topology analysis. IEEE Computer Graphics and Applications. 2000;**5**:46-51

[32] Shinagawa Y, Kunii TL. Constructing a Reeb graph automatically from cross sections. IEEE Computer Graphics and Applications. 1991;**6**:44-51

[33] Shinagawa Y, Kunii TL, Kergosien YL. Surface coding based on Morse theory. IEEE Computer Graphics and Applications. 1991;**5**:66-78

[34] Harvey W, Wang Y, Wenger R. A randomized O (m log m) time algorithm for computing Reeb graphs of arbitrary simplicial complexes. In: Proceedings of the Twenty-Sixth Annual Symposium on Computational Geometry. 2010. pp. 267-276

[35] Tierny J, Gyulassy A, Simon E, Pascucci V. Loop surgery for volumetric

meshes: Reeb graphs reduced to contour trees. IEEE Transactions on Visualization and Computer Graphics. 2009;**15**(6):1177-1184

[36] Doraiswamy H, Natarajan V. Efficient algorithms for computing Reeb graphs. Computational Geometry. 2009;**42**(6):606-616

[37] Doraiswamy H, Natarajan V, Doraiswamy H, Natarajan V. Output-sensitive construction of Reeb graphs. IEEE Transactions on Visualization and Computer Graphics. 2012;**18**(1):146-159

[38] Doraiswamy H, Natarajan V. Computing Reeb graphs as a union of contour trees. IEEE Transactions on Visualization and Computer Graphics. 2013;**19**(2):249-262

[39] Wyvill G, McPheeters C, Wyvill B. Data structure for soft objects. The Visual Computer. 1986;**2**(4):227-234

[40] Carr H, Snoeyink J, van de Panne M. Flexible isosurfaces: Simplifying and displaying scalar topology using the contour tree. Computational Geometry. 2010;**43**(1):42-58

[41] Bajaj CL, Pascucci V, Schikore DR. The contour spectrum. In: Proceedings of the 8th Conference on Visualization'97. 1997. pp. 167-173

[42] Carr H, Brian D, Brian D. On histograms and isosurface statistics. IEEE Transactions on Visualization and Computer Graphics. 2006;**12**(5):1259-1266

[43] Meyer M, Scheidegger CE, Schreiner JM, Duffy B, Carr H, Silva CT. Revisiting histograms and isosurface statistics. IEEE Transactions on Visualization and Computer Graphics. 2008;**14**(6):1659-1666

[44] Takeshima Y, Takahashi S, Fujishiro I, Nielson GM. Introducing topological attributes for objective-based visualization of simulated datasets. In: Volume Graphics, 2005. Fourth International Workshop on. 2005. pp. 137-236

[45] Weber GH, Bremer P-T, Pascucci V. Topological landscapes: A terrain metaphor for scientific data. IEEE Transactions on Visualization and Computer Graphics. 2007;**13**(6):1416-1423

[46] Beketayev K, Yeliussizov D, Morozov D, Weber GH, Hamann B. Measuring the distance between merge trees. In: Topological Methods in Data Analysis and Visualization III. Cham, Switzerland: Springer; 2014. pp. 151-165

[47] Bunke H, Riesen K. Graph edit distance: Optimal and suboptimal algorithms with applications. Analysis of Complex Networks: From Biology to Linguistics. 2009:113-143. https://onlinelibrary.wiley.com/doi/book/10.1002/9783527627981

[48] Saikia H, Seidel H-P, Weinkauf T. Extended branch decomposition graphs: Structural comparison of scalar data. Computer Graphics Forum. 2014;**33**(3):41-50

[49] Thomas DM, Natarajan V. Symmetry in scalar field topology. IEEE Transactions on Visualization and Computer Graphics. 2011;**17**(12):2035-2044

[50] Laney D, Bremer P-T, Mascarenhas A, Miller P, Pascucci V. Understanding the structure of the turbulent mixing layer in hydrodynamic instabilities. IEEE Transactions on Visualization and Computer Graphics. 2006;**12**(5):1053-1060

[51] Carr HA, Tierny J, Weber GH. Pathological and test cases for Reeb analysis. In: Topology-Based Methods in Visualization 2017 (TopoInVis 2017). 2017

[52] Edelsbrunner H, Harer J, Patel AK. Reeb spaces of piecewise linear

mappings. In: Proceedings of the Twenty-Fourth Annual Symposium on Computational Geometry. 2008. pp. 242-250

[53] Carr H, Duke D. Joint contour nets. IEEE Transactions on Visualization and Computer Graphics. 2013;**20**(8):1100-1113

[54] Duke DJ, Hosseini F, Carr H. Parallel computation of multifield topology: Experience of Haskell in a computational science application. In: Proceedings of the 3rd ACM SIGPLAN Workshop on Functional High-Performance Computing. 2014. pp. 11-21

[55] Duke DJ, Hosseini F. Skeletons for distributed topological computation. In: Proceedings of the 4th ACM SIGPLAN Workshop on Functional High-Performance Computing. 2015. pp. 35-44

[56] Duke D, Carr H, Knoll A, Schunck N, Nam HA, Staszczak A. Visualizing nuclear scission through a multifield extension of topological analysis. IEEE Transactions on Visualization and Computer Graphics. 2012;**18**(12):2033-2040

[57] Schunck N, Duke D, Carr H, Knoll A. Description of induced nuclear fission with Skyrme energy functionals: Static potential energy surfaces and fission fragment properties. Physical Review C. 2014;**90**(5):54305

[58] Schunck N, Duke D, Carr H. Description of induced nuclear fission with Skyrme energy functionals. II. Finite temperature effects. Physical Review C. 2015;**91**(3):34327

[59] Geng Z, Duke D, Carr H, Chattopadhyay A. Visual analysis of hurricane data using joint contour net. In: Computer Graphics and Visual Computing (CGVC). 2014

[60] Edelsbrunner H, Harer J, Natarajan V, Pascucci V. Local and global comparison of continuous functions. In: Visualization, 2004. Washington DC, USA: IEEE; 2004. pp. 275-280

[61] Edelsbrunner H, Harer J. Jacobi sets of multiple Morse functions. Foundations of Computational Mathematics. 2002;**8**:37-57

[62] Chattopadhyay A, Carr H, Duke D, Geng Z. Extracting Jacobi structures in Reeb spaces. In: EuroVis-Short Papers. 2014

[63] Chattopadhyay A, Carr H, Duke D, Geng Z, Saeki O. Multivariate topology simplification. In: arXiv Prepr. arXiv1509.04465. 2015

[64] Strodthoff B, Jüttler B. Layered Reeb graphs of a spatial domain. In: Bookl. Abstr. EuroCG. 2013. pp. 21-24

[65] Bachthaler S, Weiskopf D. Continuous scatterplots. IEEE Transactions on Visualization and Computer Graphics. 2008;**14**(6): 1428-1435

[66] Zomorodian A, Carlsson G. Computing persistent homology. Discrete & Computational Geometry. 2005;**33**(2):249-274

[67] Carlsson G, Zomorodian A. The theory of multidimensional persistence. Discrete & Computational Geometry. 2009;**42**(1): 71-93

[68] Carlsson G, Singh G, Zomorodian A. Computing multidimensional persistence. In: Algorithms and Computation. Berlin, Heidelberg, Germany: Springer; 2009. pp. 730-739

[69] Bremer PT et al. Topological feature extraction and tracking. Journal of Physics: Conference Series. 2007;**78**(1):12007

[70] Suthambhara N, Natarajan V. Simplification of jacobi sets. In: Topological Methods in Data Analysis and Visualization. Berlin, Heidelberg, Germany: Springer; 2011. pp. 91-102

[71] Nielson GM, Hamann B. The asymptotic decider: Resolving the ambiguity in marching cubes. In: Proceedings of the 2nd Conference on Visualization'91. 1991. pp. 83-91

[72] von Bitter Rucker R. Geometry, Relativity and the Fourth Dimension. New York, NY, USA: Dover Publications; 1977

[73] Hollasch SR. Four-Space Visualization of 4D Objects. Tempe, Arizona, USA: Arizona State University; 1991

[74] Weigle C, Banks DC. Complex-valued contour meshing. In: Proceedings of the 7th Conference on Visualization'96. 1996. p. 173-ff

[75] Weigle C, Banks DC. Extracting iso-valued features in 4-dimensional scalar fields. In: Proceedings of the 1998 IEEE Symposium on Volume Visualization. 1998. pp. 103-110

[76] Bhaniramka P, Wenger R, Crawfis R. Isosurfacing in higher dimensions. In: Proc. Vis. 2000. VIS 2000 (Cat. No.00CH37145). 2000

[77] Harvey W, Wang Y. Topological landscape ensembles for visualization of scalar-valued functions. Computer Graphics Forum. 2010;**29**:993-1002

Chapter 5

From Data Chaos to the Visualization Cosmos

Chao Tong and Robert S. Laramee

Abstract

Data visualization is a general term that describes any effort to help people enhance their understanding of data by placing it in a visual context. We present a ubiquitous pattern of knowledge evolution that the collective digital society is experiencing. It starts with a challenge or goal in the real world. When implementing a real-world solution, we often run into barriers. Creating a digital solution to an analogue problem create massive amounts of data. Visualization is a key technology to extract meaning from large data sets.

Keywords: data visualization, real world challenge, data chaos, digital solution

1. Introduction

Data visualization is a general term that describes any effort to help people enhance their understanding of data by placing it in a visual context. Patterns, trends and correlations that might go undetected in numeric on text-based data can be exposed and recognized easier with data visualization software [1]. **Figure 1** represents a ubiquitous pattern of knowledge evolution that the collective digital society is experiencing. It consists of six basic constituents. It starts with a challenge or goal in the real world. The goal could be to build or optimize a design, like a car or computer. The start could be a challenge such as reaching a new level of understanding or observing a behavior or phenomenon rarely or never seen previously. The goal could be running a successful business and making a profit. We all have real world goals and challenges. We all have new understanding and knowledge we would like to obtain. We all have things we would like to build, create, and optimize.

When trying to build something we generally know that whatever it is, it can theoretically be built in the real-world. For example, cars and structures can be built out of raw materials and components with the right tools. We also know that observations can be made, in general, by being in the right place at the right time, either personally or with recording equipment. Experiments can generally be conducted with the appropriate equipment. New levels of understanding can generally be obtained if we hire enough of the right people.

However, when implementing a real-world solution, we often run into barriers. Cars and structures are extremely expensive to build and may also require a long-term investment. Observations may be very expensive, very difficult, or even impossible. Some observations interfere with the very behavior or phenomena they are trying to study. Recording equipment may be too expensive or cause logistical problems. Equipment for experiments is generally very expensive. This is especially true if the equipment is specialized or for very small or very large-scale investigations. Also, hiring people for new understanding may not be feasible due to expense. A full-time research assistant costs 100 K GBP per year under current funding agency full economic costing (FEC) requirements in the UK. Real-world solutions are generally very expensive or not feasible at all. Some real-world solutions are impossible.

It is because of the high cost of real-world solutions that collectively, as a society, we turn to digital solutions to address our challenges and goals. The dotted line in **Figure 1** separates the real, physical, or analogue world on the left side from the digital world on the right. We all look to the digital world for the answers to our questions. "There must be an app for that." or "What app can be built to solve this problem?" is the collective thinking in this day in age. Society looks towards digital solutions for their real-world problems to deliver the user from the dilemma they may face. People believe that software is less-expensive to build than objects in the real world. The virtual world should be more feasible than the physical or analogue world. And this is true in many scenarios.

However, creating a digital solution to an analogue problem introduces new challenges. In particular, digital solutions, including software, create massive amounts of data. The amount of data digital approaches generate is generally unbounded. Software and storage hardware is less and less expensive with time. Thus, users collect, collect, and collect even more data. This is the point at which the knowledge evolution pipeline of **Figure 1** becomes interesting. Large collections of complex data are not automatically useful. Extracting meaningful information, knowledge, and ultimately wisdom from large data collection is the main challenge facing the digital world today. The collection of essentially unbounded data is what we term data chaos. Collecting and archiving data without careful planning and well thought out information design quickly or slowly results in a chaotic data environment. Those who collect data are generally not yet aware of how difficult it is to then derive useful insight and knowledge from it.

On the other hand, the knowledge that visualization is a key technology to extract meaning from large data sets is rapidly spreading. This is one solution to the data chaos. In the early years of data visualization as a field, say the first 10 years, from 1987 to 1997, data visualization was considered very niche. Not many people knew about it nor knew of its existence. It is only since around the turn of the century that

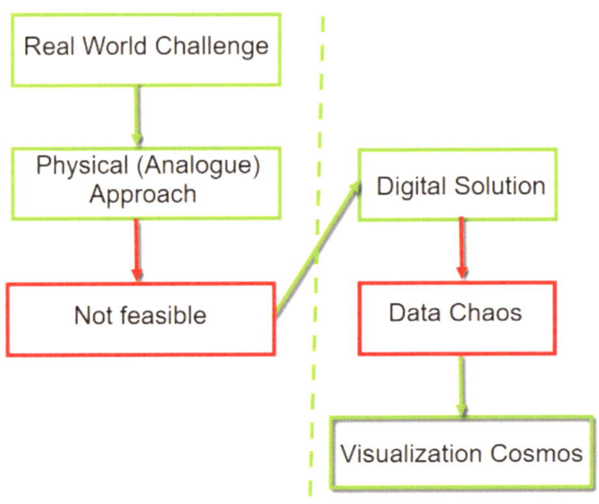

Figure 1.
A ubiquitous pattern of knowledge evolution. Here we present the model of our collective thought process.

word started to spread. In the 2000s the first main-stream news stories including the phrase 'Data Visualization' were published. Nowadays, the field has come a long way from obscurity to breaking into the main stream. Its presence and importance as a field is starting to become understood. Word is spreading that a data visualization community exists and that this is a topic a student can study at university.

That's the basic pattern of knowledge evolution. The rest of the chapter provides concrete examples of these six stages from real-world challenges to the visualization cosmos. The focus is on the last two stages: from data chaos to the visualization cosmos.

2. The universal big data story (and quandary)

We can find this pattern everywhere. It does not matter where we look. We can see in computational fluid dynamics. Physicists and astronomers are facing these dilemmas. It's not possible to study all the stars and black holes physically. We see this pattern with marine biologists, biochemists, psychologists, sociologists, sport scientists, journalists, and those studying the humanities. We see this evolution with government councils, banks, call centers, retail websites, transportation. The list is virtually endless. You can experience this yourself as you collect your own photos. People like to collect things. This is another contributing factor to the data chaos. A person may not even have a goal to reach or a problem they are trying to solve. They just like to collect.

3. The visual cortex

Data visualization uses computer graphics to generate images of complex data sets. It's different from computer graphics. "Computer graphics is a branch of computer science, yes, but its appeal reaches far beyond that relatively specialized field.

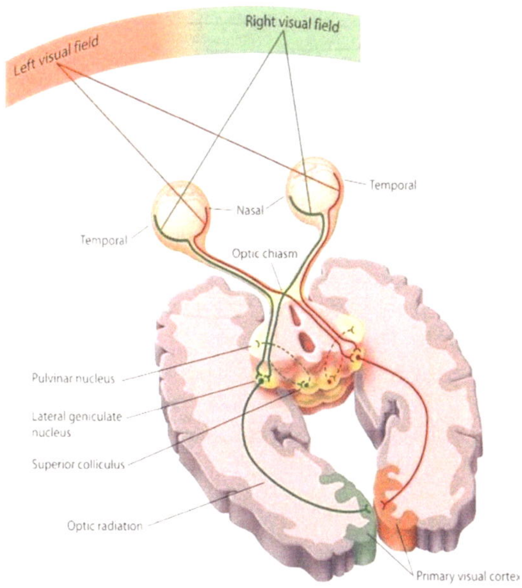

Figure 2.
Several billion neurons are devoted to analyzing visual information.

In its short lifetime, computer graphics has attracted some of the most creative people in the work to its fold," from the classic textbook "Introduction to Computer Graphics" by Foley et al. [2]. Visualization tries to generate images of reality. Visualization exploits our powerful visual system. We have several billion neurons dedicated to our visual processing and visual cortex [3]. See **Figure 2**.

The numbers of neurons are not very meaningful unless we put them into context. We have 8% of the cortex dedicated touch and 3% dedicated to hearing. We have anywhere from 4 to 10 times of our cortex dedicated to visual processing than the other senses. It makes sense to explore the visual processing power in our brains as opposed to the other senses. It's dedicated to processing color, motion, texture, and shape.

4. Visualization goals

Data visualization has some strengths and goals itself. One of the goals of data visualization is exploring data. This may be the case when the user does not know anything about their data set. They just want to find out what it looks like and its characteristics.

Users search for trends or patterns in the data. Exploration is for the user that's not very familiar with the dataset. Visualization is also good for analysis: to confirm or refute a hypothesis. An expert may have collected the data for a special purpose and would like to confirm or refute a hypothesis or answer a specific question. Visualization is also effective for presentation.

When our exploration and analysis is finished we can present the results to a wider audience. Visualization is also good for acceleration i.e. to speed up something such as a search process. This is often a decision-making process or knowledge discovery process. We can see things that were otherwise impossible.

5. Example: visualization of call center data

Let's look at this first example of this pattern of knowledge evolution. This is from a business context. One of Swansea University's industry collaborators is called QPC Ltd. They are an innovator in call center technology. Their goal is to understand call center behavior and to increase understanding of calls and all the activities that occur inside a call center. The call centers are staffed with many agents and the agents are answering hundreds of thousands of calls every day. How can we increase our understanding of all those events and what is happening inside of a call center?

We theoretically could go down the analog or physical route. We could hire more people that stand and observe what's happening in the call center and attempt to take notes to enhance understanding. Or maybe CCTV could be used to try to film everything that's going on. These analogue solutions will be very expensive and not very practical. The analog solution to hire more people for just observation is not practically feasible and will cost too much money.

So QPC Ltd. chose the digital solution. They decided to implement an event database. The database logs all events in the call center: who called, when they call, how much time they spend navigating menus inside the interactive voice recognition system (IVR), how long they spent in the queue before speaking to an agent, whether or not they abandon their call, which agent they spoke to, and how long they spoke to each agent etc. That digital solution in the form of a database stores of millions events every day. A call center generates lots of activities. The UK employs over a million people in call centers or about 5% of its workforce are employed in call centers [4]. It's a large market.

How do we take the chaos of call center data and visualize it to make sense of it? We can use a treemap as one of the ways to visualize call center events. See **Figure 3**. The treemap is a hierarchical data structure. We start with an overview of the data and then zoom in down to different levels of detail. In this case, the size of the rectangles is initially mapped to call volume. The different hours start from midnight to midnight again. We can see when the call center opens and when the call volume increases and reaches its maximum at around lunchtime. Then it starts to descend again.

Color is mapped to the percentage of abandoned calls by default. We can notice call centers trying to avoid abandoned calls. We can observe a big increase in abandoned calls in the evening right after dinner around 7 pm–8 pm. The user can map the calls to different colors at different costs. They can also map the colors to different kinds of events for example abandoned calls or successful calls.

We can also navigate the treemap. We can zoom in smoothly and see more details. We can zoom in to single hour and each rectangle represents a single call. We can visualize individual calls and how long they take. There is a call that lasted 2 h. The unusual calls that last long time jump right out. Probably they spent a long time with an agent—a very dedicated agent spent a long time trying to solve a customer problem. The users can use a clock interface to smoothly zoom and navigate each hour. The software features a smooth zooming and panning operation and with the clock showing. The user does not get lost.

We can easily see which hours we are observing even when we zoom in. We can zoom in even further, 1 h is broken up into 10-min intervals and then those 10-min intervals are broken up into single minute intervals. We also see a standard histogram on the left which represents the data and provides an overview. Each bar represents a 10-min interval. Color is mapped to some data attribute chosen by the user in this case the average call length which we can see up in **Figure 3**. We can see, suddenly during, the evening average call length increases, and we can see over the day the average call length increases throughout the day as an overall trend.

The treemap features a fine level of detail. Each rectangle can represent a single phone call and, in this case, how long each call lasted. At the top level are not individual calls. Each rectangle represents an hour and then each hour is broken

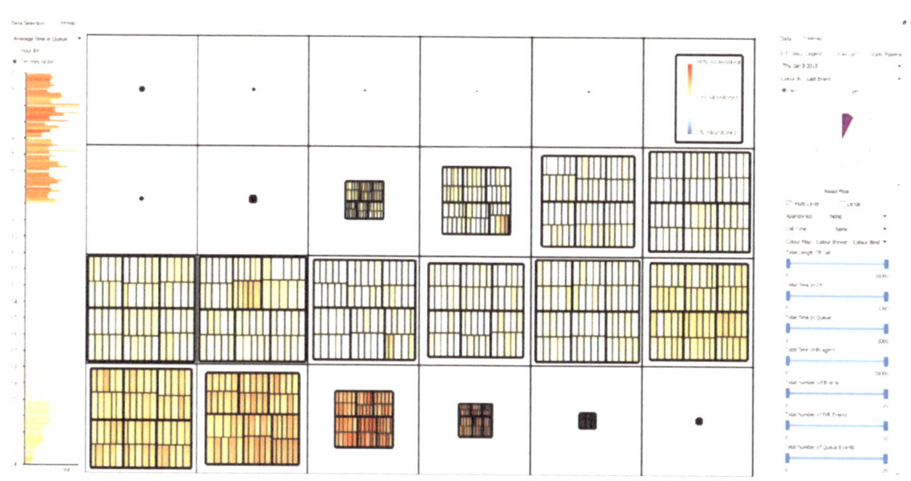

Figure 3.
Visualization of call center data. Image courtesy of Roberts et al. [4].

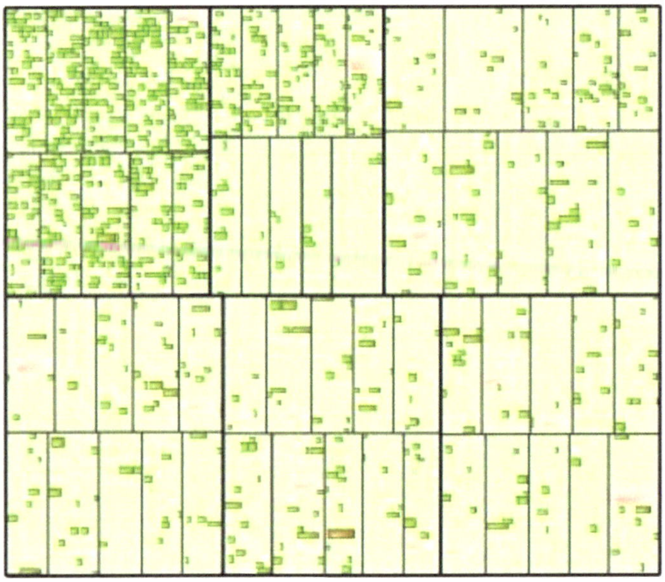

Figure 4.
Focus + context filtering feature of call center data. Image courtesy of Roberts et al. [4].

up into 10-min blocks. So we have 6, 10 min blocks and then each time in the block is broken up into individual minutes. This is an exciting project because this is the first time that QPC Ltd. have ever seen overview of the call center activity in any way shape or form. As soon as we see the overview we can easily make observations about the call center volume about the increasing level of abandon calls. The average call length is also increasing as we examine the day.

We can filter calls using different sliders. This is the analytical part of the process. This is an example of focus and context visualization. See **Figure 4**. We focus on the calls that spend a longer time in a queue.

We can focus on the inbound calls because call centers have inbound calls and outbound calls. These can be filtered by completed calls. We can combine filters in different ways.

We can click on an individual call and then obtain the most detailed level of information like how much time the caller spent in the IVR navigating menus, how much time they spent queuing and how much time they spent talking to agents. We have two different queuing events, an agent event, a second agent event, back in the queue, back to another agent, back into the queue again. That is a complicated phone call. That is the lowest level of detail. We can also see the type of call in this case a consult call as it shows the number of events, one IVR event for queuing events and four different agent event.

One detailed view shows that the proportion each event as a unit proportion because sometimes the events disappear when they're too short for a traditional version.

6. Example: investigating swirl and tumble flow with a comparison of techniques

Computational fluid dynamics is the engineering discipline of trying to predict fluid flow behavior: fluid motion as it interacts with geometries like cars, ships, or airplanes [5, 6]. If we want to understand how fluid will interact with a surface one way to do, is to build an actual surface and build a flow environment and to visualize the flow with smoke or die or other substances. This is something fluid engineers do. This is a field of engineering. But it is very expensive. Just try a test flight and then attempt to visualize the air flow around the wings with smoke. This is a very expensive experiment. There are analog solutions. Can we come up with a digital solution that makes this investigation more feasible to accelerate the engineering and make it less expensive? That is the inspiration behind computational fluid dynamics (CFD).

Here's an example of combustion chamber in an automobile engine (**Figure 5**). The engineer's goal is to obtain a perfect mixture of fuel-to-air. The way the engineers propose to do that is to create this helical motion inside the combustion chamber (**Figure 5** left) and for the diesel engine example the ideal pattern for the mixture of fluid flow is a tumble motion about an imaginary axis pointing out from the page (**Figure 5** right).

We can build a real physical solution, but it saves time and money to go through a digital process first before we build real solutions. We do not need to build as many real solutions. The digital solution is computational fluid dynamics. As we know in computational fluid dynamics, the number one challenge is the amount of data that simulations generate which is at the gigabyte and terabyte scale. CFD simulations run from weeks to even months even on high performance computing machines. How can we use visualization to make sense of this massive amount of CFD data?

Let's look at some data visualization solutions for CFD data, visualizing the swirl and tumble motion. See **Figure 6**. This is the tumble motion example so those are called path or short path lines in the flow direction and the color is mapped to crank angle. We have a piston head moving up-and-down a thousand cycles per minutes (at the bottom—not shown).

We can also use vortex corelines a combination of these green paths of vortex core lines: centers of swirling flow. See **Figure 7**. When combined with particles, the particles show flow behavior around the vortex cores. This is what we call feature-based flow visualization—looking for special features in the flow [5, 6]. We can visualize the flow at the surface itself using so-called critical points. That's a sink and that's a saddle point. And then there are some curves that connect the different points. Those are special kind of streamline called separatrices and they show the topology of flow.

Topology is a skeletal representation of the flow. We can see the time-dependent topology of the flow-sinks, the sources, and the vortex corelines. The vortex core lines are tubes in the middle. We also see a separatrix on the boundaries of the surface and they are animated over time. That's a slow-motion version of time. It

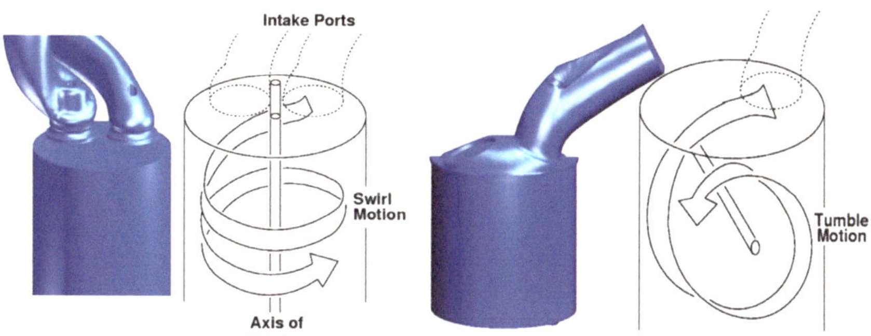

Figure 5.
Investigating swirl and tumble flow with a comparison of flow visualization techniques. Image courtesy of Laramee et al. [5].

Figure 6.
Pathlets visualizing tumble motion of flow. Image courtesy of Garth et al. [6].

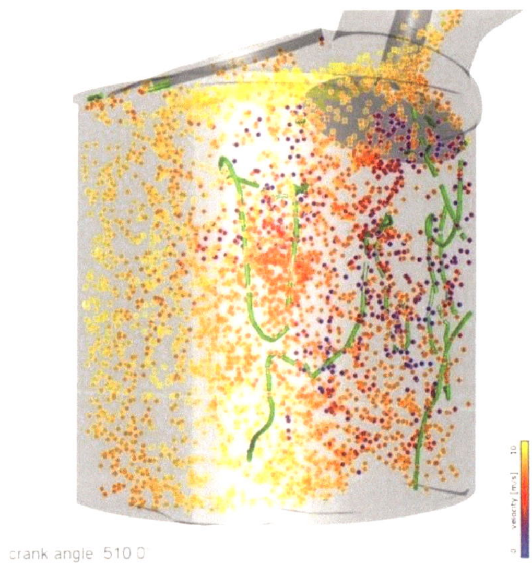

Figure 7.
A hybrid visualization of particles and vortex core lines. Particles swirling around vortex cores aid the visualization of vortex core strength. Image courtesy of Garth et al. [5, 6].

is slowed down quite a lot. In reality this is inside of the engine and it's moving up and down hundreds of times per minute. We can also use a volume visualization of the fluid flow specifically for the vortices so the vortices are the areas of swirling motion. The red is mapped to one direction of circular flow and blue the other.

The idea is to visualize the swirl and tumble motion. In this case the tumble motion is about an imaginary axis that points out at the viewer just like a tumble dryer. We can observe an axis pointing out and downwards to the left of the ideal axis. It's a very unstable axis of rotation. That is what these visualizations show an unstable rotational axis.

The computation fluid dynamicists see this and they observe this is not the ideal tumble motion. There's a little bit of tumble motion right around the perimeter of the geometry but as soon as we look in the center we still see some swirling motion but it's very far from the ideal kind of tumble motion they strive for. They have to make some modifications to the geometry to try to realize the best mixing possible. And here this is also not the ideal swirl motion. The motion is off-center. Again they have not achieved their target of the ideal motion. That's what these visualizations show. They show the difference between the actual and predicted motion.

One of the things that the engineers like to know is where precisely the flow is misbehaving. They know what they want to see and what they expect to see. They like to see visualizations that highlight unwanted behavior. That's what all users want to see. In fact, that could be in the knowledge evolution pipeline. One of the things QPC would like to see where the abandoned calls are and when people are not behaving properly. Here the engineers can see where the flow does not behave properly. This is one of the strengths of visualization—to show when and where behavior go wrong.

7. Example: visualization of sensor data from animal movement

The next example is from marine biology. Marine biologists would like to understand marine wildlife and how marine wild life behaves. One of the challenges that they face is deep sea underwater diving. How do you study animals that dive deep underwater for hours or even days at a time? How is that possible? Theoretically the solution might be to follow the animal. That might be kind of an approach. But there are some problems with that. People cannot just dive a few kilometers underneath the water. They can try to build submarines or similar but to try to follow a cormorant or tortoise in a submarine is not a very practical solution. It's not feasible, very expensive, and the analog solution is one of those cases where the observation itself influences the behavior we are trying to study.

Marine biologists look to the digital world for a solution. They use sensor devices at Swansea University called a daily diary [7]. They actually capture the animals like a cormorant. They attach the digital sensor or maybe more than one digital sensor to the subject and then release it. See **Figure 8**.

Then they recapture the sensor a few hours or a few days later. They remove it from the animal and they study the information that it collects about the local environment. It collects information on acceleration, local acceleration, local temperature, pressure, ultraviolet light, and a few other properties. Another challenge currently is that GPS does not work underwater at great depths. It's not possible to just plot a path naively in a dead reckoning fashion the same way we can for land animals.

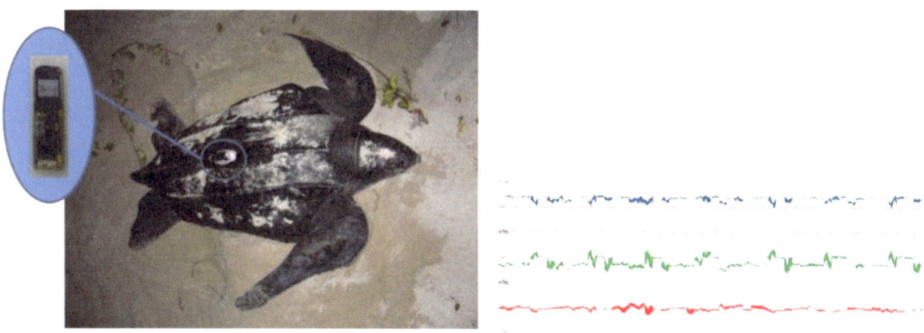

Figure 8.
Visualization of sensor data from animal movement. Image courtesy of Grundy et al. [7].

However, when the user get this data this is what it looks like (see **Figure 8** right). This is a tiny little piece of what it looks like. They plot, for every attribute, magnitude versus time. Acceleration Magnitude is on the y-axis and time is on the x-axis. They claim they can infer animal behavior based on these wave patterns. They can look at a wave pattern and say that it looks like the animal is diving or the animal hunting.

But you can see that that's not easy. This is only a few seconds of data. If you plot the day's worth of data in this fashion, it will wrap around a building a few times. The acceleration has three components: x, y, z. These are three components decoupled. In reality they form a vector in 3-space.

The marine biologists asked us if we can drive visualizations that facilitate the understanding of marine wildlife behavior. We have a standard visualization coupled with a new visualization (see **Figure 9**). In the new visual design we can see the geometry of the animals and how the animal is oriented immediately. What Grundy et al. did was reintegrate the x, y, z components of the acceleration and plot them in spherical space rather than time versus amplitude space. And they map the unit vectors onto a sphere and can immediately infer animal behavior. They can also map pressure to the radius. **Figure 9** shows the animal swimming at the surface and then the pressure increases. Pressure mapped to radius represents diving behavior and the diving behavior is very easy to notice. Now that is visualized in spherical space we can observe swimming, hunting, searching behavior. This spherical space is interactive so that we can rotate, zoom, and pan at different angles.

Figure 10 presents a spherical histogram. The vectors are binned into unit rectangles and the more time an animal spends in a given posture at that orientation,

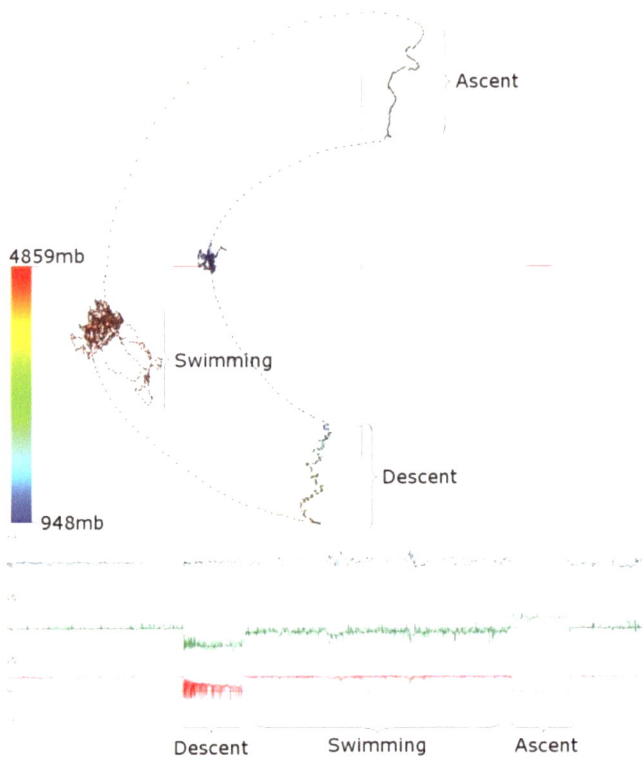

Figure 9.
Spherical visualization of sensor data coupled with standard visualization (bottom). Image courtesy of Grundy et al. [7].

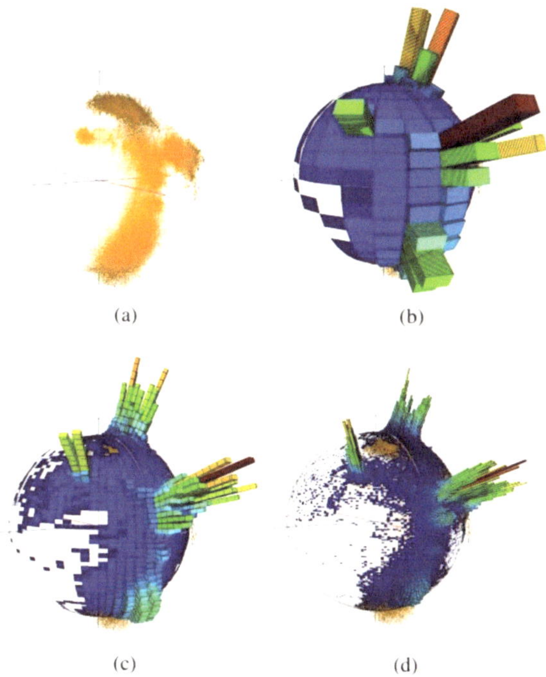

Figure 10.
Spherical histogram of sensor data. Image courtesy of Grundy et al. [7].

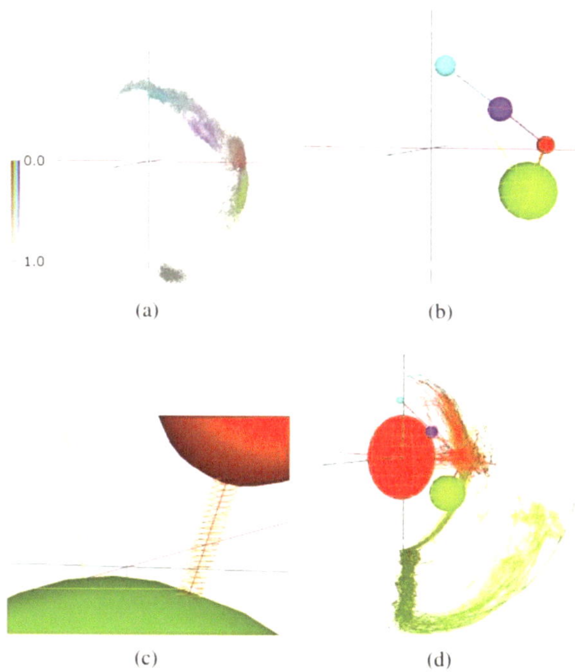

Figure 11.
Utilizing data clustering methods of sensor data. Image courtesy of Grundy et al. [7].

the longer histogram bin. We can see the postures and the states that the animals spend a long time in. Rather than focusing on all of the time, the user chooses a special region and then the region is plotted up close in the left-hand corner. The user can cluster the vectors into different groups (see **Figure 11**). Assigning each data point to a group that represents some interesting aspect of the animal behavior. The user can adjust the probability of any data sample belonging to one of the clusters. These are clusters of animal postures calculated using *K*-means clustering. Grundy et al. can represent clusters as spheres and then connect the spheres or the postures with edges that represent transitions from one orientation to another successively. We can observe the transitions between various states and postures. We can see the most popular or dominant states. That information pops up immediately.

8. Example: visualization of molecular dynamics simulation data

The goal here is to understand biology at the molecular level. There are analog approaches and solutions to this challenge. Biologists run experiments at the molecular level and try to understand behavior of molecules using experiments and nuclear magnetic resonance spectroscopy. These machines and experiments are very expensive.

The whole field of computational biology attempts to address this challenge in the digital world because it's much less expensive than the analog world. As with any simulation data all the simulation experts generate massive amounts of data. They try to use the latest high-performance computing machines.

This is the interaction of lipids and proteins. See **Figure 12**. That's what this simulation data shows and Alharbi et al. [8] develop some visualization software to enhance understanding of this. These holes are protein and then the paths are lipid trajectories. See **Figure 12**. The computational biologists attempt to visualize the interaction between trajectories and the proteins.

Alharibi et al. are trying to develop visualizations to help computational biologist understand the data with a special focus, in this case, on path filtering. Given the massive number of trajectories hundreds of thousands or millions of trajectories

Figure 12.
Visualization of molecular dynamics simulation data. Image courtesy of Alharbi et al. [8].

over multiple time steps, is it possible to select a subset of those trajectories based on interesting properties that help the biologists understanding the behavior? Alharibi et al. develop tools for filtering and selection of these trajectories to try to understand behavior. One example is just changing the time step of the simulation or filtering the path by its length. They can focus on shorter paths or on longer paths. They can slide the filter over to long paths or the long trajectories.

The user can filter the paths based on other characteristics. They chose a few properties that they hope will be interesting for the computational biologists. One property is curvature. There are highly curved paths.

The atom trajectories are actually three dimensions, but they're limited to a layer analogous to the biosphere such that the z dimension is relatively small compared to the x and y dimensions. They can visualize projected 2D space or the volumetric 3-space. The user can experiment with 2D versus 3D. The standard visualization packages for this are constrained to a two-dimensional plane and they're generally not interactive.

9. Conclusion

This chapter presents a ubiquitous model of knowledge evolution witnessed at a collective level by a society deeply involved with the digital world. It presents a theory supported by a number of case studies ranging from the call center industry, to automotive engineering, to computational biology. It sets the stage for data visualization as a vital technology to evolve our understanding of data and the world it describes to the next level. It will be exciting to witness how this model and pattern evolve over time.

Author details

Chao Tong* and Robert S. Laramee
Visual and Interactive Computing Group, Swansea University, Swansea, UK

*Address all correspondence to: tcjohn2046@gmail.com

References

[1] Data Visualization Definition. Available from: https:// searchbusinessanalytics.techtarget.com/ definition/data-visualization [Accessed: 2018-06]

[2] Foley JD, Van Dam A, Feiner SK, Hughes JF, Phillips RL. Introduction to Computer Graphics. Vol. 55. Reading: Addison-Wesley; 1994

[3] Ware C. Information Visualization: Perception for Design. Elsevier; 2012

[4] Roberts R, Tong C, Laramee R, Smith GA, Brookes P, D'Cruze T. Interactive analytical Treemaps for visualization of call centre data. In: Proceedings of the Conference on Smart Tools and Applications in Computer Graphics. Eurographics Association; 2016. pp. 109-117

[5] Laramee RS, Schneider J, Hauser H. Texture-based flow visualization on isosurfaces. Constance, Germany: IEEE TCVG Symposium on Visualization (VisSym); 19-21 May 2004:85-90

[6] Garth C, Laramee RS, Tricoche X, Schneider J, Hagen H. Extraction and visualization of swirl and tumble motion from engine simulation data. In: Topologybased Methods in Visualization. Springer; 2007. pp. 121-135

[7] Grundy E, Jones MW, Laramee RS, Wilson RP, Shepard EL. Visualization of sensor data from animal movement. In: Computer Graphics Forum. Vol. 28. No. 3. Wiley Online Library; 2009. pp. 815-822

[8] Alharbi N, Laramee RS, Chavent M. Molpathfinder: Interactive multidimensional path filtering of molecular dynamics simulation data. In: The Computer Graphics and Visual Computing (CGVC) Conference. Vol. 2016. 2016. pp. 9-16

Chapter 6

New Graphical Password Scheme Containing Questions-Background-Pattern and Implementation

Bulganmaa Togookhuu, Wuyungerile Li, Yifan Sun and Junxing Zhang

Abstract

Security of authentication is needed to be provided superlatively to secure users' personal and exchange information, since online information exchange systems have been developed according to internet speed. Therefore, aim of the chapter is to develop current graphical password scheme based on recall, create and implement a new graphical password scheme composed of three layer verification. We programmed our scheme in order to use in section of anonymous information exchange system and user's registration of trading chat room. While we conducted survey on user by accessing participant to our system lied in participants' local network and we analyzed in accordance with the average length of their created password and statistical significant of entropy bit. From the survey of total participants, our scheme has statistical significance, furthermore it was proved that it can secure form a variety of attacks as entropy bit was high.

Keywords: graphic password, user authentication, QBP scheme and implementation

1. Background

Textual password mechanisms are the most commonly used, however with known weaknesses. The weaknesses include user fallibility in memorizing long or complicated passwords and the security risks posed by the use of short simple passwords.

One motivation for examining the application of graphical schemes is that humans have a remarkable capability to remember pictures. Second background of category is that most of the recall-based graphical passwords systems developed.

In addition, another motivation for this research is "what we build is what we remember more". Current forms of commonly promoted graphical passwords can be divided into three general categories: recognition-based systems, cued-recall systems and recall-based systems.

1. For the recall-based category, Jermyn et al. proposed a scheme, called "draw-a-secret (DAS)". A user asked to draw a simple picture on a 2D grid. During authentication, the user asked to re-draw the picture. If the drawing touches the same grids in the same sequence, the user is authenticated.

2. For the recognition-based scheme called pass point, users have to recognize their pass image on images when they see them again. When they register, the user either provides their own images or chooses from a collection provided by the system.

3. In a recall-based system, the user has to recreate their pass image every time they log in. This is similar to a written signature used to sign documents. A cued recall-based system provides cues to users to help them repeat their initial actions, such as selecting points in an image each time they log in.

One common problem for graphical passwords is the shoulder surfing problem: an on-looker can steal a user's graphical password by watching in the user's vicinity.

Therefore, the aim of this chapter is to develop existing graphical password scheme based on one's memory, create and implement a new graphical password scheme that is composed of three-layer verification.

1. Scheme of secret question and answer based on text

2. Scheme of choosing image based on recognition

3. Scheme of creating password using drawing based on remembering

We programmed our scheme in order to prove its superiority comparing with existing schemes. We attend on user survey that participants access to our system on local network. It was according to the average length of their created password and statistical significance of entropy bit. From the survey results of total participants, we find that our scheme is statistically significant, furthermore it was proved that it can secure a variety of attacks due to its high entropy.

2. Related work

Since it has been proved that images are easier to recall than text phrase, some people have been suggested graphical password as an alternate. Dirik et al. [1] classified the graphical password into three systems such as pure recall-based systems, recognition-based systems and cued recall-based systems [2]. People who use recall-based password system have to remember their password to access to system. Furthermore, one of the most famous studies of recall-based techniques was offered by Jermyn et al. [3].

The system of Govindarajulu et al. [4] that used doodles as recall-based systems, requires expensive equipment, such as a touchpad and digitizing tablet that are attached to a computer and users also need each time to learn how to use the system. Recognition-based graphical passwords systems lie in a variety of images used and user either chooses benefits provided by the system or provides their own images.

Hai Tao [5] draws the password using grid intersection points instead of grid cells. In addition, this scheme gave users a chance to select longer passwords and use colors, both resulting in greater password complexity than in DAS scheme. Hatching et al. [6] selected pass image one–by-one with the same sequence by drawing the curve starting from the given image (red rectangle) and ended the image marked with a green rectangle. While Thorpe et al. [7] set the selected location "X" marker near his or her previously chosen location, they used Google Maps and large password space.

3. CRS graphical password scheme and concepts

Numerous researchers are concentrating and writing research papers on authentication and security of contemporary information system. One of them is shoulder surfing attacks unlocking smart phone used for everyday life [8–10]. Users, however, can create strong entropy or password consisted of long bits in terms of any single system, which is difficult to remember. Thus, we have improved security of Pass-Go scheme, added secret questions, answers and background image, processed and implemented a new scheme to solve the problem. It called "Questions-Background Image-Pattern (CRS)".

Thus, we have improved security of Pass-Go scheme, added secret questions, answers and background image, processed and implemented a new scheme to solve the problem.

Main activity of CRS runs according to principle choosing node dots instead of partition, similarly Pass-Go scheme. It can be easy not only to use but also beneficial to remember while it may create strong and complex password because of inserting background image in the view, similar to BDAS pattern.

Our CRS is consisted of triple verification parts to secure safety of password superlatively. For instance:

1. Scheme of secret question and answer based on text

2. Scheme of choosing image based on recognition

3. Scheme of creating password-using drawing based on remembering

when user has created a password only generated a new version by adding the traditional scheme of question and answer contained password feature to scheme of a graphical password. It can be used in web site of information trading and authentication phrase of trading chat room.

To refer systems based on modern web using graphical password scheme rarely, graphical password scheme based on recognition (selecting Chinese characters and various images) is used in authentication section of large searching systems like Android OS for smart phone pattern lock, Google and Baidu. Some psychologists assume that human brain remember graphical information better than others [11]. One of the researches revealed that how authentication and unlocking process influence based on phone user's behavior.

In accordance with Dual Coding Theory, cognition is consisted of two different sections such as nonverbal and verbal systems [12, 13]. Thus, user will pass following steps to register using our scheme. After choosing questions and answers to them and inserting optional background image behind the grid, graphical password is created and appeared. Then user will create password by connecting points lying on the board and drawing shape using straight line.

Therefore, we processed scheme which secures safety of password, combined with practice and implemented as a result of studying graphical password space theory.

Our proposed idea is devoted to advertising web site of anonymous information trading containing feature of test-based and graphical password and authentication section of trading chat room that trades secured file to contract safely. CRS scheme can be protected from various attacks since there is no personal information about the users on the website. While designing the scheme, we established a graphical password scheme, which is easy to use, interesting and strong, integrated by adding both BDAS [20] based on recall and Pass-Go [5] graphical password scheme to password like traditional test-based having secret questions and answers.

In our CRS scheme, there are 25 points on the 5 × 5 board and user connects points and draws optional image on free position using straight line. It is possible to mark eight directions freely by striking at least more than four points. Drew path from start point to end will be numbered 1–25. When reproduce, user need to select point drawn in previous step correctly and draw to end by recall previous imagination. This requirement aimed at creating strong drawing graphical password, which provides system security. Our scheme, thus, is divided to 5 × 5 grids, developed like consisted of overall 25 points and implemented in authentication section of system based on web. User should register in accordance with following scheme. The CRS scheme flow diagram (**Figure 1**).

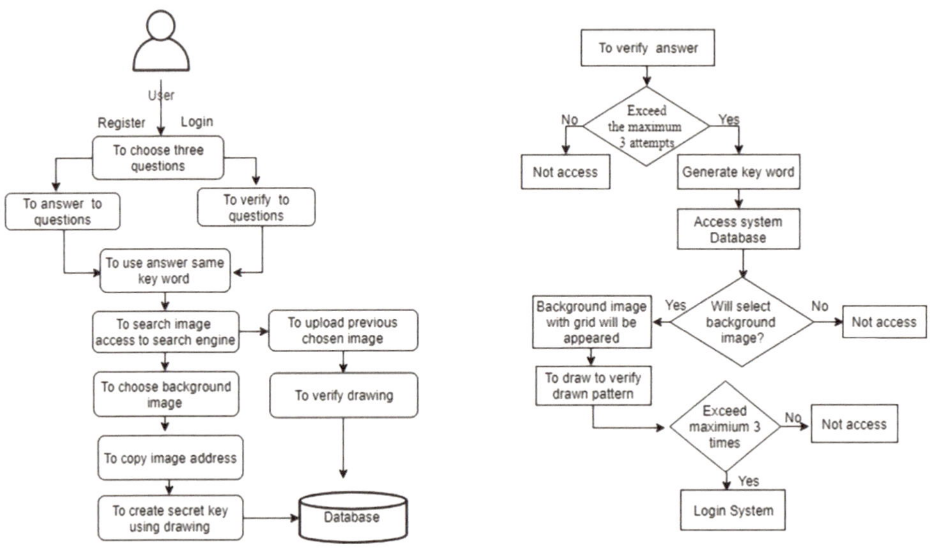

Figure 1.
Register, login process, questions and answers verification.

4. Main unit of the CRS graphical password scheme

User accesses authentication page of system, selects and answers three of variety questions. Using secret question and answer in system authentication section is responsible for increasing overall bits' size of password. In order to prepare secret question and answer based on a user, we should obey prohibited regulations of international telecommunications industry and the FCC's Customer Proprietary Network Information (CPNI) that do not contain questions about user's personal information.

Password does not contain user's personal information such as e-mail address, surname, birth date, user's registration number and phone number. The password requires answers that are easy to memorize, adamant in terms of time, has feature to cover public, is difficult to guess and provides security. If attackers capture user's weak answer, they will experience trouble in every step to guess graphical password created by secret drawing or next step verification.

- We are required consisted of long characters question and answer from user to provide answer security. Therefore, we decided that minimum of answer character is ≤ 4, maximum of accepting answer can be composed of ≤ 10–26 (letter, number and exclusive character) when answer using collocation.

- Questions will appear with original text as user selects question. However, answer was saved by cryptographic hash function. Users need to select a new question's pack again and create new one if they forget answer. If session idle both will warn to answer secret question within 3 minutes and move to next step (verification step).

- Images which are appropriate to find using chosen three answers of questions like keywords will be revealed separately on three web guides from system base.

- When user selects one image and copies location code (copy image address), the image will be the background image of our system and inserted behind grid. One advantage of this way helps to deceive attackers who want to obtain background image.

- Board inserting background image should be 5×5 grids while user will select from 25 points on 2D board and draws by pen-up from start to endpoint under pen-drag movement. User need to connect under following rule and mark as a line.

    - User needs to select at least four points.

    - Previous points can choose by concurring, if there is no neighbor point.

    - It confirms to connect points using only straight line and mark.

    - It is impossible to select by jumping over next point without choosing previous point.

    - User can create number of optional images in free positions.

The fifth step improves Pass-Go scheme, solves haziness of graphical imagination and increases password space.

5. To verify secret drawing

Firstly, to select and answer to secret question; secondly, to create password using drawing; thirdly, to create graphical password using secret drawing.

As a result of integrating cited-above sections, password containing long bit will be created. Bit size is different depending on choice of answer's character. The bit entropy has estimated by traditional test-based password (if it is ≤28 bits, they are greatly weak; if it ≤28–35 bits, they are weak; if it is ≤36–59 bits, they are probable; if it ≤60–127 bits, they are strong and if it ≤128+ bits, the greatly strong).

When users register to system firstly, they will pass following steps such as answering to secret question, inserting background image behind blank grid and creating password using drawing on it. To access, user reproduces previous 2 steps and verifies by reproducing previous secret drawing. After checking every step in any condition on system, user can access successfully, if every data is correct in verification steps. If access right was canceled after making over three attempts in any step, user needs to create from beginning. Although it is a strict requirement, it can provide security.

5.1 Implementation and evaluation

We used JavaScript, node.js and developed in condition of Linux operating system. User ID, password and other associated data will be saved in SQLite database in server part. The proposed CRS can be used in website of information trading and user authentication section of trading chat room. We solved the problem and processed scheme, which is easy to use by improving current password scheme and providing security superlatively. Implementation step is consisted of following sections.

1. User can select three of optional questions and answer to them.

2. User finds image from search engine using answer like keyword.

3. User selects only one image and inserts background image.

4. A 5 × 5 grid consisted of 25 points, which will be inserted on background image.

5. For probability of selecting overall points, n-gram probability will be estimated based on Markov model.

6. Selected points will be estimated by probability of decreasing sequence.

7. We program under scheme and estimate password strength according to user's study.

5.2 Implementation interface

Our scheme will select intersection of two-dimensional coordinate pairs based on recall instead of cell. In this section, we will study start and end of safe pattern and sub-pattern, and then estimate through Shannon's entropy. Mono-grams will be probability of selected N-point on overall pattern to estimate entropy of start and end point. To estimate N-gram, we have estimated probability of X point appearing in entropy pattern or Nth using N-1 point and used (**Figure 2**).

The conditional entropy is estimated by Shannon's formula [21] (F_N: N-gram entropy).

$$F_N = -\sum_{i,j} p\left(b_{i,j}\right) \log_2 p\left(b_{i,j}\right) + \sum_{i} p(b_i) \log_2 p(b_i) \quad (1)$$

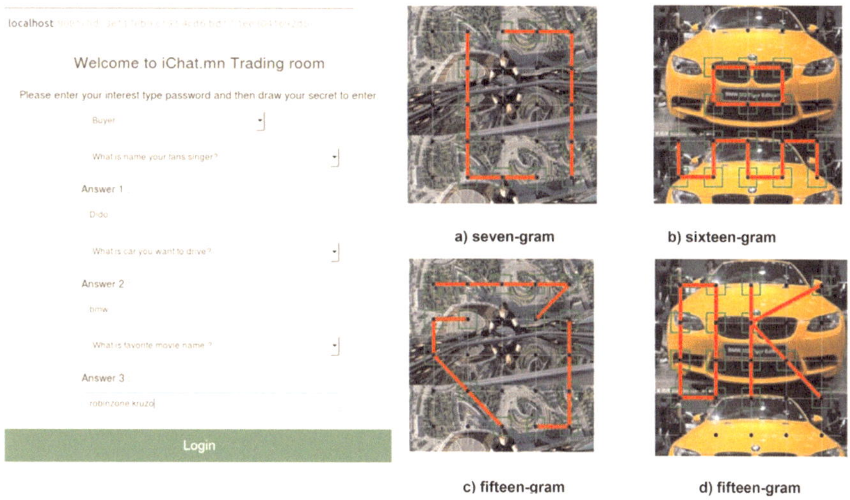

Figure 2.
CRS—graphical password user interface. (a) User selects questions and answers, (b) most frequently drawn points, (c) few drawn points and (d) average drawn points.

Here, b_i is (n − 1) grams, b_j is an arbitrary point which has not been chosen and $P(b_{i,j})$ is the N-gram probability of $b_{i,j}$. It can be marked from upper left corner by representing "0" like modern android phone lock. For example, it will be expressed by following formula if bigram is b_i = 01″ and b_j = 02″.

$$p(b_{i,j}) = p(''012'') = \frac{\#of\ occurrences\ of\ trigram\ ''012''}{sum\ of\ occurrences\ of\ all\ trigrams} \quad (2)$$

While guessing entropy, [22, 23] is one metric that can be used to measure the strength of a (password) distribution. The method determines possible connections from start point to the endpoint.

6. Used in research methodology

6.1 Point selection (N-grams)

To create a password using our scheme, overall 25 points will connected and it will be marked by sequence of line. Thus, we will concentrate on N-gram and establish probability having the strongest feature. In general, it is assumed that N-gram having enough probability is significant to estimate probability taken from [24].

For instance, when n = 2, we need to learn 25 × 24 = 600 values and we need to learn when n = 3 in terms of our scheme 25 × 24 × 23 = 13,800 (slightly less than). Users usually created secret drawing using 15-gram and 16-gram probability. It was observed that a number of points' choices were increased and image was drawn by enough long straight because of inserting background image.

6.2 Selecting start and end points

More than half of research participants (51.1%) started upper left or left side to choose start point. In addition, over half of our research participants chose upper left point as a start point and it is related to their mother language written from upper left point.

For all points having the same probabilities, the entropy of start point is 2.35 bits to a maximum of $\log_2^{61.9}$ bits compared. For male participants, they selected car and football images, set them on background image and expressed chosen average 18 spaces of start and end with much longer. For female participants, they selected flower and a variety of brands, set them on the background image and chose few points (chosen point's average is 19.3). To observe choice of end point, they chose lower right points more than other and estimated probability is 2.75 entropy bit. From the survey, the most frequent path is upper left and bottom right point and it defined that we can estimate points' averages.

6.3 Measure strength of password

Our password scheme is consisted of combination of character and graphical password and create strong password, which is longer over 128 bits by adding length of user's answered character. Many researchers aimed at measuring password strength using a variety of measuring methods. Thus, we measured password entropy established by text-based and graphical password separately.

$$H = \log_2 N^L = L \log_2 N = L \frac{\log N}{\log 2} \tag{3}$$

Password entropy measures condition that is impossible to predict and use longer password based on character (lowercase, uppercase and special characters). Optional password strength is measured by information entropy. Furthermore, possible password and number are expressed by $\log_2$ and every characters creating password will be processed independently. Therefore, information entropy of optional password is estimated by following [25] H-formula:

N is possible number of character, L is number of string (character) on the password and H is measurement of bit.

6.4 To encode graphical password and full password space

User-drawn image will be encoded by sequence of intersections represented by two dimensional coordinate pairs. Points passed through intersection points using mouse will be numbered by value from 1 to 25.

The length of password is the number of coordinate pairs except pen-ups in the password encoding. Based on a password with length L, where adding one point (P2) or increasing the last through a unit of any directions of the least 3 and most 8, with length of L + 1, a new password will be made. When L = 1, the password has the minimal length.

$$PS \leq S1 + S2 + S3 + DP\,(n) \tag{4}$$

PS is the size of the full password space, S1, S2 and S3 are sizes of the textual passwords from users' responses to random challenges, and DP(n) is the size of the graphical password space.

7. CRS-new graphical password scheme evaluation

Since it is difficult to assess security of graphical password, we studied usage part and indicated survey result by conducting survey on our scheme. Because of it, user can choose numerous points to create password and chance to guess by attackers will be decreased.

We chose participants from foreign students living in school campus using collecting data method and gave instruction as how to execute work before conducting on survey. Then participants accessed to system existed in local network and created graphical password will be used to pass to trading chat room. We indicated demographical survey of overall participant and creating graphical password. Total 50 participants aged from 25 to 55 were enrolled in our survey and they worked and spent over 8 hours on computer-related internet environment.

7.1 Login time

We estimated average of spent overall time when total participants accessed to login and verification system. Unlocking the devices, users on average spent 2.6 minutes each day as presented by Harbach et al. [26]. Thus, we assumed that 3 minutes are enough to pass trading chat room and verify based on the survey. Depending on ability of computer usage, we deducted participants who spent more than 3 minutes from survey result.

In addition, the maximum of three answers that participants chose and answer to questions in the first step is 191.3 bits and the minimum of three questions is 23 bits. We divided participants' created password into long and short sections and we studied length of password using Kruskal-Wallis [27] tests method in terms of sufficiency changes of successful login. Consequently, short secret has $H(5) = 19:31$, $p<:02$ significance and long secret has $H(5) = 15:91$, $p<:04$ significant.

When classifying participants based on sex and comparing the length of straight drawing graphical secret, male created line with 18 average lengths whereas female created line with 19.3 average lengths. Participants chose 15-gram, 20-gram and created secret drawing and the maximum repeated of 15-gram is 14%. When estimated, the average of creating secret of participants is 1.08 sec. The maximum is 2.5 minute while the minimum is 0.30 sec.

7.2 Success rate

Due to the aggregate attempts from an individual, the success rate is determined on average with successful logins. During re-register and verifying 15 minutes after participants created secret successfully, different results were revealed. Total time to recall authentication is within 3 minutes and there are the maximum of three-access right to insert password three times in every verification sections. Total participants recall differently on three sections of verification: Recalling as one access is 38%, recalling as two accesses is 30%, recalling as three accesses is 16% and participant who cannot pass access number exceeding is 16%.

7.3 Password strength

The theoretical password space of a graphical password scheme is a security strength indicator defined by the total number of possible passwords. Recall schemes based on drawing shapes have been shown to suffer from tentative patterns [7, 28].

In cited-above survey, we suggested that bit entropy must be high to secure password used in system from attackers. Therefore, we shown our new graphical password scheme based recall entropy bit (**Figure 3**).

Table 1 shows the capacity of total bits of the graphical password based on traditional textual password and recalling by comparing them. For instance, when

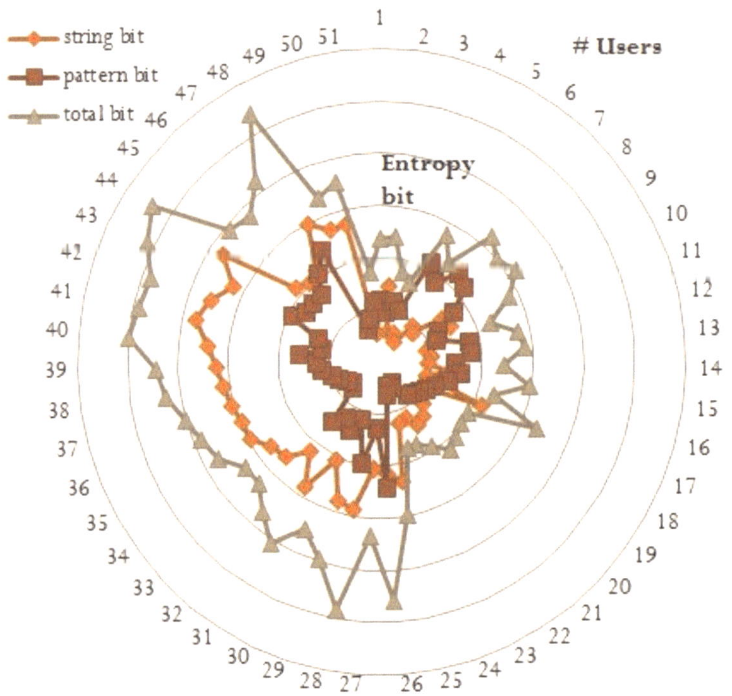

Figure 3.
Recall entropy bits and user number.

	Textual password (95^n) [13]	DAS [28]	BDAS [29]	Pass-go [5]	Proposed CRS scheme
Bits	$95^{28} = 2^{129}$	$2^{96.2}$	2^{76}	2^{256}	$\leq 2^{271}$

Table 1.
Compare full graphical password bit space.

we choose a textual password that has maximum 28 characters, it is worth with 129 bit. Maximum capacity of DAS scheme based on recalling was 96.2 bit while maximum capacity of BDAS model was worth with 76 bit. Maximum capacity of Pass-go model developed by improving DAS model based on initial recalling is 256 bit. Our CRS scheme was developed by combining advantages of above-given models and its maximum capacity is worth 271 bit. As a result, it can help to reduce risk of attack.

From view, **Table 1** proposed most bit-size for CRS scheme. We suggested that bit entropy must be high to secure password used in system from attackers.

8. Conclusions

This chapter provides introduction to graphical password, its study, new type of graphical password design, its implementation and its results. For large system, main problem is secret verification. Indeed, it is thing being developed to hammer out solution in any time. We proposed graphical password, based on user's habit and interest, is easy to use and created password consisted of strong entropy bit. Studied usability aspect of CRS graphical password by providing users with CRS graphical password and monitored their graphical password creation and their utilization.

Total of 50 users have participated in this study, and analyzed their time spent in CRS graphical password creation, how long they could remember it and strength of the password. Thus, it can secure a variety of attackers such as traceability of fingerprint smudges, dictionary, shoulder attack, brute force attack and so on. We can use our scheme providing password security for checking mail, service of social network messenger, internet bank, website of trading organization, training website and authentication of a variety of devices.

Author details

Bulganmaa Togookhuu[1], Wuyungerile Li[2], Yifan Sun[2] and Junxing Zhang[2*]

1 School of Engineering and Technology, Mongolian University of Life Sciences, Ulaanbaatar, Mongolia

2 College of Computer Science, Inner Mongolia University, Huhhot, Inner Mongolia, China

*Address all correspondence to: junxing@imu.edu.cn

References

[1] Dirik AE, Birget. Modeling User Choice in the PassPoints Graphical Password Scheme. In: Symposium on Usable Privacy and Security (SOUPS); 2007

[2] Delprato D. Mind and its evolution: A dual coding theoretical approach. The Psychological Record. 2009;**59**(2): 295-300

[3] Jermyn I et al. The design and analysis of graphical passwords. In: The 8th USENIX Security Symposium; Washington, USA. 1999. pp. 1-15

[4] Noor Ain R, Singh D. Early learning malay vocabulary using speech technology: Dual code theory approach. In: Proceedings of the International Conference on Electrical Engineering and Informatics. 2011

[5] Tao H. Pass-Go: A New Graphical Password Scheme. Canada: Master of Applied Science, Electrical and Computer Engineering, University of Ottawa; 2006

[6] Davis D, Reiter K. On user choice in graphical password schemes. In: USENIX Security Symposium. 2004

[7] Wagner P. Cryptanalysis of a cognitive authentication scheme (extended abstract). In: IEEE Symposium on Security and Privacy. 2007

[8] Oorschot J et al. Graphical dictionaries and the memorable space of graphical passwords. In: USENIX Security Symposium. 2004

[9] Shokarev A, Kostyuchenko E. User authorization in the picture password system with application of digital watermarks. In: 2016 Dynamics of Systems, Mechanisms and Machines (Dynamics). 2016

[10] Ventura N et al. An approach password graphic for access control web. In: Conference on Information Systems and Technologies (CISTI). 2016

[11] Skinner G. Cyber security for younger demographics, a graphic based authentication and authorisation framework. In: IEEE Region 10 Conference (TENCON). 2016

[12] Dunphy P, Yan J. Do background images improve draw-a-secret graphical passwords. In: Proceedings of the ACM Conference on Computer and Communications Security (CCS); New York, USA. 2007

[13] Shannon C. Prediction and entropy of printed English. Bell System Technical Journal. 1951;**30**(1):50-64

[14] Cachin C. Entropy measures and unconditional security in cryptography [PhD dissertation]. https://cachin.com/cc/papers/d.pdf

[15] Sebastian Uellenbeck MD. Quantifying the Security of Graphical Passwords: The Case of Android Unlock Patterns, Publication Security, Human Factors, ACM, 978-1-4503-2477-9/13/11; 2013

[16] Wikipedia. Password Strength. Available from: https://en.wikipedia.org/wiki/Password_strength

[17] Marian H et al. A field study of smartphone (un)locking behavior and risk perception. In: Symposium on Usable Privacy and Security. Menlo Park, CA: USENIX Association; 2014

[18] Li L, Tsai M. Notice of retraction
a study on quality traceability of transmission assembling based on Kruskal-Wallis method. In: International Conference on Quality, Reliability, Risk, Maintenance, and Safety Engineering (QR2MSE). 2013

[19] Thorpe J, Salehi-Abari A. Usability and security evaluation of geo pass, a geographic location-password scheme. In: Symposium on Usable Privacy and Security (SOUPS); Newcastle, UK.

[20] Password Choosing and Using Security Questions. Available from: https://www.owasp.org/

[21] Shannon C. Prediction and entropy of printed english. Bell System Technical Journal. 1951;**30**(1):50-64

[22] Yan P. Do background images improve "draw a secret" graphical passwords? In: ACM Conference on Computer and Communications Security (CCS). 2007

[23] Bulganmaa T et al. New graphical password scheme containing questions-background-pattern and implementation. Procedia Computer Science. 2017;**107**:148-156

[24] Needham M. Prudent engineering for cryptographic protocols. IEEE Transactions on Software Engineering. 1996;**22**(1):6-15

[25] Karabey I, Akman G. A cryptographic approach for secure client—server chat application using public key infrastructure (PKI). In: International Conference for Internet Technology and Secured Transactions (ICITST). 2016

[26] Naman S, Khandelwal P. Two factor authentication using visual cryptography and digital envelope in Kerberos. In: International Conference on Electrical Electronics Signals Communication and Optimization (EESCO). 2015. pp. 1-6

[27] Micali S. Distributed split-key cryptosystem and applications, U.S. Patent No. 6026163; 2000

[28] Sudha M, Thanuja T. Randomly tampered image detection and self-recovery for a text document using Shamir secret sharing. In: IEEE International Conference on Recent Trends in Electronics, Information & Communication Technology (RTEICT). 2016

[29] Yang X, Xiao M. Verifiable secret sharing and distributed key generation based on hyperplane geometry. In: 2nd International Symposium on Dependable Computing and Internet of Things (DCIT). 2015

[30] Yingli Z. A Key Escrow Scheme to IOT Based on Shamir. ChengDu, China: Research Institute Electronic Science and Technology, University of Electronic Science and Technology of China; 2013